POETRY AND THE COMMON LIFE

M.L. Rosenthal

SCHOCKEN BOOKS • NEW YORK

First published by Schocken Books 1983
10 9 8 7 6 5 4 3 2 1   83 84 85 86
Copyright © 1974 by Oxford University Press
Foreword copyright © 1983 by M. L. Rosenthal

Library of Congress Cataloging in Publication Data
Rosenthal, M. L. (Macha Louis), 1917–
  Poetry and the common life.
  Reprint. Originally published: New York: Oxford
University Press, 1974.
  Bibliography: p.
  Includes index.
  1. Poetry—History and criticism. I. Title.
PN1075.R6   1983   808.1   82–16913

Manufactured in the United States of America
ISBN 0–8052–3851–4 (hardcover)
    0–8052–0738–4 (paperback)

For permission to reprint passages from the works indicated grateful acknowledgment is made to the following:

W. H. Auden. Excerpt from "Lullaby" is Copyright 1940 and renewed 1968 by W. H. Auden; excerpt from "Shield of Achilles" is Copyright 1952 by W. H. Auden. Both from *W. H. Auden: Collected Poems* by W. H. Auden, edited by Edward Mendelson. Excerpt from "Spain, 1937" is Copyright 1940 and renewed 1968 by W. H. Auden. Reprinted from *The English Auden: Poems, Essays, and Dramatic Writings 1927–1939* by W. H. Auden. All by permission of Random House, Inc. and Faber and Faber Ltd.

Imamu Amiri Baraka (LeRoi Jones). Excerpt from "Black Art" from *Black Magic Poetry 1961–1967* by Amiri Baraka. Copyright © 1969 by LeRoi Jones. Reprinted by permission of Ronald Hobbs Literary Agency.

George Barker. "To My Mother" from *Collected Poems* by George Barker is reprinted by permission of Faber and Faber Ltd.

John Berryman. Excerpt from "Dream Song #29" from *The Dream Songs* by John Berryman. Copyright © 1959, 1962, 1963, 1964, 1969 by John Berryman. Reprinted by permission of Farrar, Straus & Giroux, Inc. and Faber and Faber Ltd.

Paul Blackburn. "The Once-Over" from *Early Selected Y Mas* is Copyright © 1972 by Joan Blackburn. By permission of Black Sparrow Press. Excerpt from "Peire Vidal" translated by Paul Blackburn by permission of Joan Blackburn.

Bertolt Brecht. Excerpt from "To Posterity" by Bertolt Brecht, trans-

for Sally Moore Gall
gratitude for clear thoughts,
disturbing questions

Contents

Foreword

My original impulse in writing *Poetry and the Common Life* was to share an open secret, an intimate sense of poetry as the one art whose materials—all the resources and nuances of language—are of the very essence of human expression. One thing that this means is that whatever goes into a poem's phrasing and rhythms and echoes and memories and reticences connects, quite directly, with everyone's subjective life. All this is totally self-evident; and yet the absolute saturation of poetry with the colors and intensities of human awareness and feeling, the dynamic structure that depends on a progression of tonalities rigorously reciprocal with our internal states, are hardly common knowledge. One wants to cross the invisible, baffling barrier that makes poetry something people "don't get" and that often makes supposed specialists in literature write and teach about everything except what actually happens in a poem.

The problem is not that poetry ought to be simpler, more popular, less "privileged"—not at all. In fact, it is the most intransigently self-contained art that is most informed by the common life. Joyce's *Ulysses*, Dante's *Inferno* teem with the world as we know it and with the dreams and desires and fears of the common imagination. What struck me as I began to write this book was how the instances flooded my mind and at every step opened up far more perspectives than I wished, for the moment, to pursue. I had only, as it were, to start with any poem I knew and in some sense loved, and the process of demonstration seemed to take care of itself. More and more poems, and more and more dimensions of my subject, presented themselves swiftly and seductively. Poetry, Eugenio Montale once wrote, is the result of "silence and accumulation." What is being accumulated (or received by "negative capability," in Keats's famous phrase) is the body of psychic configurations we all share with our fellows despite every private idiom—converted, of course, into its linguistic and aesthetic distillations and thus liberated from the rut of the merely literal. This is the richest meaning of "symbolism."

The revelatory delight and terror of this process, this objectifying of what would otherwise remain the hardly conscious flickerings of introspective and dreaming reverie, must certainly become obvious once its existence is recognized. When we read novels of earlier generations such as *Middlemarch* and *Jude the Obscure*, we not only find passages of poetry used as epigraphs; we also find them employed in dialogue to suggest whole contexts of mutual understanding—that is, as the coinage of emotional exchange. In such dialogue one indispensable condition obtains: the desire to get at the naked realities of felt meaning. Perhaps these realities are too intractable, too challenging, for minds of the sort William Carlos Williams says are "like beds always made up." Nevertheless, they provide the only experiences, apart from our most basic pleasures, that make life interesting. In this realm the questions are always open questions and the answers always volatile, tentative, and possibly most disturbing.

I hold to something like a pure aestheticism (very idiosyncratic, and to be explained to my more patient friends on some occasion that will be, for them, inescapable), for it permits the whole of life to swarm in through the back door and suffer imaginative transformation before it has the chance to swarm out again. Rigor of form, communion with the marvelous achievements of the past, are the necessary discipline for artists of any kind who would wring the utmost felt meaning from the plastic materials at their disposal.

"Felt meaning" is a quality of form, and it is only the greatest poets who constantly touch the essential nerves of our emotional life. The ending of *Paradise Lost*, so simple and touching, is so not only because of the mighty issues proclaimed from the start and the pathetic allegory that accounts for death and suffering. It also connects with the recurrent human state of disastrous loss and the need to resume as best one can. Everyone must pass through the ordeal:

> Some natural tears they dropped, but wiped them soon;
> The World was all before them, where to choose
> Their place of rest, and Providence their guide:
> They hand in hand with wand'ring steps and slow,
> Through Eden took their solitary way.

Or take this moment in *King Lear*:

> Pray do not mock me;
> I am a very foolish fond old man,
> Fourscore and upward, not an hour more nor less;
> And, to deal plainly,
> I fear I am not in my perfect mind.

—A heartbreaking moment in the play, but also a reverberation from how many moments in how many lives and ages, especially with its lightly garrulous and wandering common colloquial touch "Fourscore and upward, not an hour more nor less" (actually comic in one aspect).

And in fact—not to start piling up instances here—I can think of no poem of memorable quality in which such endlessly human reverberations, their sources clearly discernible everywhere in our common condition, do not command both the work's structure and our sense of how it counts. It is for this reason, I think, that this book "wrote itself" in the way the luckier poems do, instructing its author in the direction it must take.

M.L.R.

April 1983

Foreword

I have sometimes felt that an unconscious conspiracy exists to keep the people from their poetry. By "their poetry" I do not mean the lyrics of popular songs and simple inspirational or political verse but the real thing, the poetry that poets themselves and their most developed readers cherish. The conspiracy is amiable enough. Critics and scholars have developed their special interests and knowledge and vocabularies, and they like talking to people who more or less understand what they mean and who appreciate the background and purpose of what they are saying.

Still, the fact remains that human life, in all its depth and variety and reality, is the province of everyone's thought, not just that of literary specialists. And human speech and awareness, rich in their idiom and range, are the lovely stuff of poetry. Human situations, human concerns, human voices make even the most sophisticated poetry the living structure that it is. I have no sentimental notion that all poetry can or should be readily understood by everyone at once. Nor do I think that the stubborn mass indifference to it will change very soon. Nevertheless, it is here for anyone's asking. What poets have to report rises from a world of experience shared with people of all conditions, people whose inward sense of life is of the same order as their own. Poets are the verbal antennae of a people. The awareness they distill and convert into the dynamics of language is somehow present in the populace at large. We neglect it at our peril.

I wish there had been a way to say the things I say in this book so directly and yet so engagingly that anyone picking it up would get the point at once of poetry's immediacy and relevancy to his or her own life. At times it seems so very simple—just listen to the voice that speaks, just let yourself be taken by the currents of feeling set going by the way a poem starts. But I know it's not that simple, any more than what goes on in most people's minds is simple. Like ordinary human experience, poetry is often uncomplicated in appearance yet rooted in deep underlying reaches of feeling and of association.

And then again I am not thinking so much of the "appreciation" of poetry as of seeing how it counts, what connections it has with what we all really are and wish to be. Every poet of interest has brooded over these connections. William Carlos Williams's *Paterson* is a straightforward assault on the issue, seeking to "unravel" and reveal a "common language" that binds poet and people together as participants in cultural communion. Wordsworth and Whitman are Williams's most famous predecessors in this search. I am not proposing a systematic theory of poetry or a pedagogical introduction or a discussion of poetic technique for its own sake. The pages that follow do contain thoughts, I am sure, that might naturally serve such purposes; but I have something plainer, happier, and in fact more revolutionary in mind. I hope these pages will help refresh the stream of modern thought about poetry by recalling that it is the poets, through their constant response to the touch of life, who are the truest spokesmen for the wide human world in which they move and dream.

M. L. R.

July 1974

1/ Poetry and Ordinary Experience

Life without poetry would, I believe, be very much less worth living. I speak of poetry now as a natural human activity and state of awareness. It is an expression of what one poet, Gerard Manley Hopkins, called "my sweating self." It belongs to the world of hunger and sex—a kind of thought, but thought felt as bodily need and energy. Poetry is filled with memories of the physical impact of feelings and sensations, including especially the impact of sound and most especially of the human voice.

John Berryman's "Dream Song 29," for instance, begins with a feeling of the *weight* of undefined guilt on a man's heart. Various remembered sensations attach themselves to his "heavy" feeling, and the voice we hear is of someone who has carried infantile misery into adulthood as an inescapable burden. It is really a mixture of two voices, that of a gravely perceptive, mature person and that of a childlike one who does not always speak grammatically:

> There sat down, once, a thing on Henry's heart
> só heavy, if he had a hundred years
> & more, & weeping, sleepless, in all them time
> Henry could not make good.
> Starts again in Henry's ears
> The little cough somewhere, an odour, a chime.

Now perhaps this is to begin from the wrong end, from poetry in relation to our griefs rather than to our joys. But just as people sometimes weep with happiness, so art measures feeling by its intensity rather than its literal object. Whatever the medium—the painter's oils, the sculptor's marble, the composer's notes and chords, the dancer's own body, or the poet's words—art converts feelings into aspects of that medium, such as shadings of color or a dancer's patterned movements; and the conversion demands a certain degree of intensity. In Berryman's poem about the depression that "sat down" on "Henry's heart," the intensity is almost the same as when Tennyson's speaker in *The Princess* says, in his very different mood of love-ecstasy:

> Now lies the Earth all Danaë to the stars,
> And all thy heart lies open unto me.
>
> Now slides the silent meteor on, and leaves
> A shining furrow, as thy thoughts in me.
>
> Now folds the lily all her sweetness up
> And slips into the bosom of the lake:
> So fold thyself, my dearest, thou, and slip
> Into my bosom and be lost in me.

Many people, I admit, lead very full lives without poetry. It is ludicrous even to mention so obvious a fact. Yet to the poet everything he knows belies that fact. All his experience, all his introspection, flow into a rhythm and design of language. When people say they do not "get" poetry, it is because they think of language as factual description and the explanation of ideas. They forget the other ways in which they themselves use it—for social cordiality, for cold rejection or irritation, for outcries of pain and excitement, for joking or "manly" obscenities or "feminine" hyperbole. Language is like color or space or pure sound. Its realm is both conscious thought and subconscious reaction to life: the touch of other personalities, for instance, and a myriad other sensations and fears and desires. These stimuli, active in every mind, create in all of us a hunger to express ourselves accurately and vividly. Words like "humorous," "racy," "dramatic," "poignant" reveal that we want our speech to have a life of its own, something much more than flat statement. So the poet is not working out of mere private eccentricity. The poetic process goes on incessantly in the minds of people who would never believe it, who are sure they have neither an interest in poetry nor the ability to grasp it. Carl Sandburg knew and loved this unconscious poetry of ordinary life—

> When I asked for fish in the restaurant facing the Ohio river, with fish signs and fish pictures all over the wooden, cracked frame of the fish shack, the young man said, "Come around next Friday—the fish is all gone today."
>
> So I took eggs, fried, straight up, one side, and he murmured, humming, looking out at the shining breast of the Ohio river, "and the next is something else; and the next is something else."
>
> The customer next was a hoarse roustabout, handling nail kegs on a steamboat all day, asking for three eggs, sunny side up, three, nothing less, shake us a mean pan of eggs.
>
> And while we sat eating eggs, looking at the shining breast of the Ohio river in the evening lights, he had his thoughts and I had mine thinking how the French who found the Ohio river named it La Belle Rivière meaning a woman easy to look at.

The first impression of this passage, from Sandburg's "Whiffs of the Ohio River at Cincinnati," is that he is telling a joke. He begins with an anecdote about the shabby waterfront scene. Soon, however, more lyrical elements are being mixed in with the earthily realistic comic ones. When Sandburg read his poems aloud, he would speak in a slow, rocking chant that gave strong emphasis to the kind of contrast here between a wild folk-buffoonery and the tones of romantic intensity. On the one side we have the prosaic but hilarious echoing of the words "fish" and "eggs" and all the American restaurant lingo and slang—"fried, straight up, one

side," "shake us a mean pan of eggs." On the other, we have
the glamour and simple delight of the repeated words "the
shining breast of the Ohio." That phrase is linked with such
others as "evening lights" and "La Belle Rivière," which Sandburg pretends to translate into "a woman easy to look at." His
lightly colloquial, yet suggestive touch of straight-faced mis-
translation combines the flippant and the lyrical elements of
the poem. So does the counterman's half-clowning, half-
prophetic wisdom ("and the next is something else"), and
so does the speaker's easy profundity ("he had his thoughts
and I had mine").

So this casual-seeming passage is actually a sharply focused
impression of a real scene with real people, and, within it, of
contrasting elements: the presence of beauty all around the
ridiculous and nearly squalid scene. Between the beginning
and the end we move from pleasant clowning to an atmosphere of dreaming. Sandburg has created a delicate dance of
mood and tone out of materials as familiar and common as the
nearest "diner" or cheap restaurant. The appeal to the eye
and the ear, the zest for common realities, in this poem make
it like a tall tale or a certain kind of comic strip. It reflects the
relish for incongruities found in all folk and popular humor.
By the end, though, its increasingly heightened atmosphere
brings something subtler and more moving into play.

Let me take another example, plainer and less exuberant.
Robert Frost's "The Investment" grows out of the lives of
New England dirt farmers of an earlier generation. Its first
two stanzas, whose phrasing is saturated with the harsh neces-
sity of those lives, are the strongest. The poem grows weaker
in its closing six lines, when the speaker draws apart from the
people whose lives he has presented to us in order to speculate
on them:

> Over back where they speak of life as staying
> ("You couldn't call it living for it ain't")
> There was an old, old house renewed with paint,
> And in it a piano loudly playing.

> Out in the plowed ground in the cold a digger,
> Among unearthed potatoes standing still,
> Was counting winter dinners, one a hill,
> With half an ear to the piano's vigor.
>
> All that piano and new paint back there,
> Was it some money suddenly come into?
> Or some extravagance young love had been to?
> Or old love on an impulse not to care—
>
> Not to sink under being man and wife,
> But get some color and music out of life?

The first two lines of this sonnet have always given me great pleasure and are the main reason I thought of "The Investment" just now. They have such a truthful, spontaneous sound, grim and wry and witty all at once, that we know they come directly out of the farm country Frost writes about. The man or woman talking this way might never call it poetry, yet he or she would be as aware as any conscious poet of style and rhythm and nuances of phrasing. Such speech has a tradition behind it. It plays with shadings of meaning ("staying" and "living"). It is colored by brutal experience, but softened against bitterness by irony and momentarily cheerful candor. The slightly drawling pace of the first line is balanced by the mock-thoughtful briskness of the witticism in the second, with the speaker playing a character role of smart countryman and coming down hard on the words "living" and "ain't."

To the person speaking in these two lines, or at least in the second, there is the release of expressing his own inner dissatisfaction in the salty, humorous phrasing of an art form: a sly, paradoxical, compressed comment on life. The form enables him to avoid self-pity. It gives the statement a springing life of its own and makes it a piece of wisdom, like a biblical proverb. Many proverbs and folk sayings, like much racy ordinary speech and many jokes, have this kind of impersonality that they share with art generally. Cruel, demeaning attitudes may be imbedded in them—as, for instance, in the saying "Fish

and visitors stink after three days"—but even in this disagree-
able instance the achievement of an unexpected association in
the form of a witticism that is also a human insight almost
makes us forget the nastiness.

Back, though, to "The Investment"—look for a moment at
the three lines beginning the second stanza. Nothing could be
simpler than these descriptive lines; they give us the literal
scene of the farmer standing amid the potatoes he has just dug
up. The words "plowed" and "digger" and "unearthed"
speak of his hard work. The phrase "Out in the plowed
ground in the cold" gently reveals his exposed, elemental existence. That he was "counting winter dinners" shows his rel-
ative poverty, for each little mound of potatoes equals one
family meal. There is a colloquial literalness in "winter dinners,"
and the phrase, though used by an observer, speaks for the
farmer himself at the same time. It shows both his hard lot and
his sturdy providence. The language, in fact, though that of an
observer—perhaps a neighbor, perhaps the poet himself—who
is recalling an experience, also manages to project the digger's
own private thoughts. At least, this is so in the first eight lines if
we disregard the rhyme and meter and the one word "vigor." We
stand there with him, knowing what he was thinking about and
what he was listening to. The passage gives us sharply clear
pictures for the eye, while the loud piano music fills an otherwise silent scene. That is to say, Frost's language isolates these
sense impressions in such a way as to make them suggest just
how a whole way of life felt to the people living it.

The rest of the poem, giving the "moral" as it were, is less
effective. It rather hammers away at us about why these poor
folk, in their "old, old house," have invested in new paint and
a piano. The speaker clearly prefers the last of the possible
explanations he suggests, and certainly it expresses the deep
human need to make life more than a routine animal struggle
for survival—to redirect and transcend it through giving it
"color and music." My main objection to this ending is that
it is such an obvious comment from "outside," whereas the

first eight lines find just the right language from "inside" the scene. The ending loses the unsentimental compassion with which the poem started, its high spirits triumphing over a low condition. As soon as the letdown begins and the poem becomes talkative rather than concretely alive, the rhyme and rhythm become awkward too. The reason is that they call attention to themselves as part of a coldly contrived device for winding up the poem. In Sandburg's "Whiffs of the Ohio River at Cincinnati," the speaker keeps himself in the scene, blending his own mood and language with those of the people around him so that the feeling that emerges contains all the tones that have built into it. In Frost's poem the speaker does this only to a tiny extent and loses touch to a great degree. It was what was discovered in the digger's life and mind, in its own terms, essentially, that made the beginning so much more telling than the end.

But my purpose in quoting "The Investment" was not really to criticize it in detail. If I may return to something elusive and infinitely suggestive in this poem, let me quote its first two lines once more:

> Over back where they speak of life as staying
> ("You couldn't call it living, for it ain't")

One reason I love these lines is that they show how much poetry is present in the voices of people to whom it would hardly occur that this could be so. The fullness of life, of the way we all feel and the way we all speak in unselfconscious moments, is the very stuff of poetry. The touchstones of our lives, and therefore of art, are vivid experiences and strong needs either gratified or thwarted. At this moment I can see from my window, after a spring rain, four orange-breasted, speckle-backed robins poking into the high wet grass. I can turn to erotic dreaming—a memory, say, of a white shoulder just above my head at some happy moment. I can summon up harsher memories: a scream from a vast apartment building late at night on a Chicago street as I passed by, or the voice of a union organizer rising hysterically in the same city after strikers were shot down outside a steel mill many years ago. Of such sights and dreams and recollections, shared by millions of people, poetry is made.

I want to stress this point. Too often poetry is thought to be impossibly far apart from ordinary human existence. Anyone's mind is a teeming gallery of sensations and memories. Housewife, murderer, plumber, schoolboy, each has a mind full of blue or gray skies, the touch or absence of love, the give and take of conversation, the filth and excitement of cities (or the seasonal shiftings of country existence or the nervous sameness of the suburbs). We all know the taste of things sweet or bland or sour, we all have known rage, we all feel the passion to recall even a painful past. A rich confusion of awareness underlies all human feeling, and the language for it surges all around us. The poet reaches into that rich confusion toward the wellspring of the surging speech of life. He must, through language alone, catch a tone, a perception, a quality of sensation and arrange a whole poem around the impulse of energy so captured.

Frost at his best was one of the masters of the art of making metrical verse based on natural speech. He used his art to catch life on the run and then tried to hold the whole sense of it intact within a formal frame. The urge to make poetry has a good deal to do with such a purpose. That is why all real poetry, even when difficult or complex, has so much to say that comes from the depths of normal life. It is always in touch with the intrinsic music of our everyday world. More than that, it reveals and identifies the realizations that make life the surprising, often exhilarating, often terrifying condition it truly is.

As soon as one gets a glimpse of this rooting of poetry in everything we know and feel and are, it stops being something alien and formidable. Or let's say it is neither more nor less alien and formidable than dreaming at night or arising in

the morning into more conscious existence. It is an invitation
to see keenly into what our dreams and thoughts are about,
like the invitation that Frost extends to us in his little poem
"The Pasture," which introduces each of his collected editions.

> I'm going out to clean the pasture spring;
> I'll only stop to rake the leaves away
> (And wait to watch the water clear, I may):
> I shan't be gone long.—You come too.
>
> I'm going out to fetch the little calf
> That's standing by the mother. It's so young
> It totters when she licks it with her tongue.
> I shan't be gone long.—You come too.

This is poetry that has a love affair with life. "The Pasture"
takes us out into the midst of country things as they are. And
though the ordinary life of most of us today may be very far
from the poem's rural scene, the pictures of the clear pasture
spring and of the cow with her calf are powerfully suggestive
even for city dwellers. The speaker is happily anticipating
what he is going to *see*, but he is also going forth into the
world's continuing tasks. You can never clean the pasture
spring once and for all, nor will the calf remain forever just
as it is now. Since the poem introduces the whole book, it is
probably meant also as an invitation to come along to whatever a lifetime of writing will have discovered. But meanwhile, and first of all, we have the gentle urging to compan-
ionship in the literal chores of the new season. Nothing rare
is promised, yet such isolation of ordinary sense impressions is
sweetly rare indeed. Frost makes a song of his invitation, using
a refrain and simple rhymes. The poem reaches gaily into the
marvels of the commonplace, with only a just possible hint of
the lifetime of labor required to clean the pasture springs and
fetch the calves and do all the other chores season after season. The irony, from that point of view, of "I shan't be gone
long" is virtually hidden in the warm strength, the friendly,
plain, colloquial speech that invites us to plunge into the realities of the physical world.

The marvels of the commonplace, which of course includes circumstances that are superficially dull or routine,
are always present to the subconscious mind at least. The normal mind can discover them merely by paying attention to
what goes on within itself in response to the realities all
around. As Marianne Moore writes in "The Mind Is an Enchanting Thing," it is also, and more accurately, an "en-
chant*ed* thing,"

> like the glaze on a
> katydid-wing
>   subdivided by sun
>   till the nettings are legion.
> Like Gieseking playing Scarlatti . . .

It reflects and refracts the light from the world around it like
the glaze on the insect's wings. More than that, it actively in-
terprets and arranges the reality it experiences, like a piano
virtuoso playing a lovely piece of music. And it is itself physical, a living function of the body that is a composite organ of
all the senses:

> the mind
> feeling its way as though blind,
> walks along with its eyes on the ground.

The thought I am insisting on here is that an essential in-
gredient of poetic vision and genius is present in all minds.
First of all, poetry draws deeply on experiences we have all
had. We may not all be familiar with the art of Scarlatti or of
Gieseking, it is true, but we have all at some time felt we were
hearing beautiful music beautifully played. We have all observed the way a katydid-wing (or a dragonfly-wing) creates
a brilliant design out of sunlight. We have all felt our minds
groping into the essence of what we are experiencing in the
way Miss Moore describes. What the ordinary reader shares
with a very subtle poet like Marianne Moore is so important
that it would be impossible for anyone to write at all without

it. I am not saying that this fact makes the achievement of any
poet perfectly easy to grasp. One may have to go along with
a demanding set of associations; and one may have to follow
the sound of a speaking voice in elusively varied modulations
and intricately patterned rhythms. But the associations are actual human associations, the voice is that of a human mind like
our own, and the rhythmic patterning in a good poem reinforces the other qualities.

Wallace Stevens, for instance, is generally held to be a
somewhat difficult poet, and in certain respects he is. But if I
quote the closing lines of his most famous poem, "Sunday
Morning," it will be seen that he is expressing a sense of life
felt by anyone who has ever opened his eyes and looked about
him. The question raised in "Sunday Morning" is whether we
can accept without dismay the fact of a world without God.
This is, after all, a question that has disturbed modern man
and has strongly affected history. Stevens does not examine it
theoretically. Instead, he imagines the state of mind of a
moderately self-indulgent, moderately meditative woman
who on Sunday morning is a little troubled by thoughts of
death and a little guilty, or at least uneasy, at her neglect of
the Sabbath. These are feelings so common they hardly need
explanation and yet so real they cannot be ignored. They
emerge in a manner that allows us to see the poem in two possible ways. We may see it as a sort of internal dialogue between two aspects of the woman's own inner self, or we
may read it as an implied dialogue between the woman and
the poet, who imagines overhearing her thoughts and who
comments on them—as if she were delivering a monologue on
the stage and he listened and then addressed his own remarks
about it to the audience. Either way, the poem begins with
the woman's natural longing to have her life, with all its richness and possibilities, persist forever. And then the position
is more and more ardently advanced—either by the woman
taking a fuller look at reality or by the poet—that the only
choice possible is a sensuous, tough-minded idealizing of life

as it is, made all the more desirable by the finality of death. The poem is at once exquisite in the way it unfolds and very close to the way many people think and feel. In the eleven lines that close the final stanza, Stevens gives a picture of man in his universe that reflects a widespread modern viewpoint:

> We live in an old chaos of the sun,
> Or old dependency of day and night,
> Or island solitude, unsponsored, free,
> Of that wide water, inescapable.
> Deer walk upon our mountains, and the quail
> Whistle about us their spontaneous cries;
> Sweet berries ripen in the wilderness;
> And, in the isolation of the sky,
> At evening, casual flocks of pigeons make
> Ambiguous undulations as they sink,
> Downward to darkness, on extended wings.

We have been brought to this point in the poem by a series of shifts of focus and tone. At the beginning, we see the woman in her home, relaxing of a Sunday morning. We follow the drift of her mind as she turns from sheer enjoyment and reluctantly begins to meditate. Because of the circumstances and her mood, presented in vivid detail, her thoughts turn to religion and to the double meaning of the Crucifixion: the blood, suffering, and death of the man Jesus, and the promise of Paradise he brought. The ideas of "Sunday Morning" sometimes grow subtle and elusive, but the images are almost always boldly clear and strike familiar notes: "late coffee and oranges in a sunny chair," "gusty emotions on wet roads on autumn nights," "this dividing and indifferent blue" (the sky). When the images are less elementary in their reference, they still evoke familiar associations. The religious meaning of Sunday summons up "the holy hush of ancient sacrifice" in the woman's mind. Romantic young girls "stray impassioned in the littering leaves." At the thought of death, the woman's mood changes "as a calm darkens among water-

lights." Stevens does not ordinarily use folk speech the way
Sandburg, or even Frost, does, but he takes a great deal of
strength from the sensuous immediacy of his images. They
appeal at the level of reverie, which has infinitely more to
do with our bodies and emotions than with logical argument.
By the end of the poem the thinking is deliberately primitive,
except for its rejection of any place for the supernatural in
the world that we know.

The closing passage—already quoted—begins with the blunt
statement that "We live in an old chaos of the sun." The earth
is an "island solitude" in space, "unsponsored" and "free" because it has no Creator. (The phrase "of that wide water" in
the fourth line of the passage refers to an earlier use of the
words "wide water" in the first stanza. There the woman's
mind goes back, in imagination, across the ocean to Palestine
in the time of the Crucifixion.) "Free" of God, our condition is still "inescapable," bound by death's inevitability. Suddenly, now, the poem turns from the trapped feeling of these
thoughts to an emphasis on certain of earth's beautiful realities: the deer that "walk upon our mountains," the quails'
"spontaneous cries," the "sweet berries," the flights of "casual
flocks of pigeons" earthward. Their presence, like our own,
is a kind of miracle though not a divinely inspired one. In this
context the word "ambiguous," used for the undulations of
the pigeons, expresses both a general thought and a precise
observation. The general thought is simply that life's purpose,
if it exists at all, is extremely unclear but that nevertheless
we cannot help reading affirmative values into life itself. This
double idea is implied by the observation that the pigeons, as
they "sink downward," do make ambiguous movements that
suggest they might change their course. Also, they extend
their wings to control their sinking movement, and that act
of controlling power gives the impression of something triumphant ("extended"). It is almost as though they were about
to soar upwards, away from the darkness and the associations
of death.

Does this impression *prove* anything? Of course not. The whole poem, despite the ideas it suggests, merely balances sets of images and feelings against one another. These are images of life's pleasures, images of the dream of God's presence among us, and images of loss and deprivation. Lyric poets often handle the sense of life's being disastrous by finding a suggestion of affirmation in the very language they choose to show their despair. To "sink downward to darkness on extended wings" is a perfect example. So too is the description through most of the closing stanza, of the delights the earth has to offer us. Such language enables the poet to "control" destiny, as it were, through seeing it affirmatively: an assertion of desired power very close to what happens in primitive ritual.

Stevens performs this "ritual" in a more sophisticated way earlier in the poem, preparing us for his final simplifications. For instance, in the third stanza he provides a whimsical mock-theological argument, at once fanciful and half serious, to justify his call for a secular, hedonistic approach to life. Stevens uses the word "Jove" in speaking of God—a usage that allows him to combine pagan and Christian references as though he were at liberty to construct his own version of such sacred tales as the Greek account of the rape of Leda by Zeus and the New Testament account of Mary's virgin pregnancy:

> He moved among us, as a muttering king,
> Magnificent, would move among his hinds,
> Until our blood, commingling, virginal,
> With heaven, brought such requital to desire
> The very hinds discerned it, in a star.
> Shall our blood fail? or shall it come to be
> The blood of paradise? . . .

Because both pagan and Christian tradition report that in the past divine beings impregnated mortals, we are now ourselves divinities by heritage. Paradise is, if only we fulfill ourselves, the physical universe we inhabit—or so we must insist.

As for the other Paradise of which various religions speak, where there is no aging and no death but only "imperishable bliss," Stevens devotes a stanza of sophisticated argument to it as well. That Paradise, he says, is "like our perishing earth" except that it is static and insipid, a mere interruption before maturing of nature's cycle. But we *need* the whole cycle of life as it is, for

> Death is the mother of beauty, mystical,
> Within whose burning bosom we devise
> Our earthly mothers waiting, sleeplessly.

Without change and death our sense responses, our dreams and desires, and our imaginations could never be felt so keenly as they are now. And so the poem proposes a kind of ritual that is not really religious and yet celebrates a "boisterous devotion to the sun"—"not as a god, but as a god might be." We belong to "the heavenly fellowship/Of men that perish and of summer morn." It is only a step from this to the very simple vision, at the end, of man and the rest of nature existing, miraculously, precariously, in "an old chaos of the sun."

This simple vision was implicit in the poem from the start, but it had to be sifted through the psychological and philosophical complexities presented in the woman's mind and examined in the dialogue. Even the parts of the poem I have called sophisticated are centered on elementary or primitive pictures. There is the picture of Jove "commingling" with human beings—that is, wandering among them and having sexual intercourse with them. There is the picture of a Paradise with the earth's own familiar fruits, the same landscapes, the same colors and atmosphere, except that it cannot change. Most striking of all, there is the picture of "our earthly mothers waiting, sleeplessly" beyond the grave—not a matter of religious faith but a piercing expression of normal human grief and desire.

Almost inevitably, then, the sensuous, emotional, and tonal texture of a poem of real interest has a primal clarity regardless of any overlay of intellectuality. Most painters paint far better than they philosophize; so do most poets. "Paint" is of course only a hint of what the poet does in a line like "Sweet berries ripen in the wilderness" or in lines like

> And, in the isolation of the sky,
> At evening, casual flocks of pigeons make
> Ambiguous undulations as they sink
> Downward to darkness, on extended wings.

What such lines present to the eye and the other senses is a focusing, such as we have all observed again and again without really seeing it sharply in just this way, of nature in action. They remind us, always surprisingly, of how dependent art must be on what it is given by common experience.

There is one blindingly obvious, very powerful psychological factor in all this. This factor is the common human longing not to let go of experience. We linger, for instance, over a beautiful scenic view, fixing it in our memories, noting more and more of its depths and shadings, considering and reconsidering it. We want to have it and keep it. But we do the same thing, usually less consciously, with less beautiful views, with persons and incidents in the ordinary course of life, and indeed with whatever somehow involves us. Even more to the point, we cannot really part with anything or anyone we love, and indeed we already long for what we have quite as much as for what we have lost. Every time we turn, as we must, from what we are attached to, the parting seems too abrupt.

This unavoidable longing of ours, pervasive and compelling, is an active motive for artistic creation. In poetry it is the urge to find language sensitive enough to evoke the impact that external realities have made on our feelings and awareness. If we go back now to the passage at the end of "Sunday Morning" (beginning "We live in an old chaos of the sun"), the sharpness of its longing has such force that it turns the poem's surface meaning right around. Surely the whole poem is less an argument for secular hedonism—though it is that too—than an attempt to cope with an overwhelming sense of loss at life's transience. The speaker's passion is to fix everything he can experience or imagine in language so keen it cannot perish. That passion—to remember and retain what inevitably we must lose—is the most powerful source of art. It is why the ancient Greeks called Mnemosyne, their goddess of memory, the mother of the Muses.

I have mentioned Mnemosyne, the Grecian goddess of memory. She was mother of the Muses, who were the goddesses both of the arts and of the sciences. In our own day we may, if we wish, still imagine her as the brooding source, present in every mind, of the desire to hold on to the full body of our lives, turning it around and around and meditating on it again and again. It is she who, in poetry, moves the poet to an acutely intimate recognition and excitement because a moment of experience has been recovered. His repossession of it will be quickened and held intact only if he discovers the right language and form; the memory will come into its own, if it does, through the dynamics of the poem. An example is D. H. Lawrence's "Piano," which catches the rush of emotional surrender as the speaker's childhood self leaps from the darkness of the forgotten life.

> Softly, in the dusk, a woman is singing to me;
> Taking me down the vista of years, till I see
> A child sitting under the piano, in the boom of the tin-
> gling strings
> And pressing the small, poised feet of a mother who
> smiles as she sings.
>
> In spite of myself, the insidious mastery of song
> Betrays me back, till the heart of me weeps to belong

To the old Sunday evenings at home, with winter outside
And hymns in the cosy parlour, the tinkling piano our
   guide.

So now it is vain for the singer to burst into clamour
With the great black piano appassionato. The glamour
Of childish days is upon me, my manhood is cast
Down in the flood of remembrance, I weep like a child
   for the past.

The scene at the start is romantic, evocative. The woman
"singing to me" performs all too well; she stirs the speaker's
memory more than she does his admiration for her or for her
talent. As her singing and playing grow more passionate, so
does the speaker's psychic return to his childhood. What
dominates him is not the glamour of the singer or of "the
great black piano appassionato" but a different "glamour,"
that of "childish days" and his mother singing to him at her
"tinkling," far inferior piano. The contrasting scenes are very
dramatically drawn. One can easily envision them as alter-
nating effects in a film. The two centers of attention—the
passionate singer and the grown man listening, and the remembered mother and her rapt little son—each strike a familiar emotional chord. The "flood of remembrance" sweeps
the speaker into his living past, yet the experience is not pure
joy. He "weeps to belong" to the old life once again—and of
course he cannot. His longing for what Stevens in "Sunday
Morning" called "imperishable bliss" has to contend with
the sure despair of realistic knowledge. But that despair is not
as drastic as it would be if memory itself were lost. Then he
would have to contend with the most severely depressed
sense of loss, of total *absence*, a misery as of having gone dead
while still remaining conscious.

   There is an interestingly apt scene in Austin Clarke's long
poem about loss of memory called *Mnemosyne Lay in Dust*.
The hero of this poem, which is autobiographical though
written in the third person, actually has had this sense of going dead. He has lost touch with his living past and is con-

fined to a mental hospital, where he has violent hallucinations. One day, suddenly, he feels himself "smaller" and back in his childhood home. For a grateful instant that is his physical reality again:

> Soon Mnemosyne had made him smaller.
> A child of seven, half gone to sleep.
> His mother was at her sewing machine,
> The shuttle clicking as she followed
> A hem. Outside, the praying garden,
> Late blossom of the elder-trees:
> Twilight was hiding from his elders,
> The toolshed, barrel, secret den.

In Lawrence's "Piano" a comparable experience is the subject of a whole poem. In Clarke's lines, though, the moment holds us as a single flare of memory within a complex psychological narrative. The gift of a minute's past happiness is for the amnesic patient a single, hardly noticed promise of return to health. It stands in gentle contrast to the torment of the hectic stanzas just before and just after the one I have quoted. This stanza, like Lawrence's "Piano," centers on the power of memory, in certain circumstances, to recover past states of existence, isolated and framed and glowing with their own life as well as with the emotion that has recalled them—something in the present moment that is shared with that past state. When we lived in that other time, we were not aware of its special radiance. The psychological life is largely a matter of accumulating a sense of oneself over the years, against which we balance a sense of the present state of our awareness and the flashes of memory that recall to us who and where we have been in the past. Marcel Proust, the greatest writer on human memory in just the sense I have been discussing, wrote: "The smell and taste of things remain poised a long time, like souls, ready to remind us, waiting and hoping for their moment, amid the ruins of all the rest; and bear unfaltering, in the tiny and almost impalpable drop of their essence, the vast structure of recollection." (Perhaps we should regard the "Overture" to *Swann's Way*, in which this comment appears, as a remarkable prose poem that throws incomparable light on the way memory is indeed the mother of poetry.)

When we are cut off from our accumulated self and its "vast structure of recollection," the resulting depression may be an acute state of psychic disorder, as in most of *Mnemosyne Lay in Dust*. No malaise is more common than depression, whether in so extreme a form or in the milder form seen in "Piano," where the distress comes from a momentary disordering of the relation of present to past. For most of us depression often is healthy and useful, exposing to us our own vulnerability so that we can reorient ourselves in sheer self-defense. For others it is a condition impossible to get rid of or, more drastically, a sign of mental disorder with the possibility of suicide never far off. A great many lyric poems express and deal with states of depression and summon up personal memories in the process. How many people there must be for whom the memories of childhood are the source of their despair, while at the same time they struggle with a sense of having failed their childhood dreams, as if they could go back to that time and right all wrongs and bring to their elders a greater happiness than their lives actually held! Randall Jarrell's poem "The Elementary Scene" is a perfect expression of this depressed state that is the mark of millions of modern lives:

> Looking back in my mind I can see
> The white sun like a tin plate
> Over the wooden turning of the weeds;
> The street jerking—a wet swing—
> To end by the wall the children sang.
>
> The thin grass by the girls' door,
> Trodden on, straggling, yellow and rotten,
> And the gaunt field with its one tied cow—
> The dead land waking sadly to my life—
> Stir, and curl deeper in the eyes of time.

The rotting pumpkin under the stairs
Bundled with switches and the cold ashes
Still holds for me, in its unwavering eyes,
The stinking shapes of cranes and witches,
Their path slanting down the pumpkin's sky.

Its stars beckon through the forest like cottages
(Homes of the Bear, the Hunter—of that absent star,
The dark where the flushed child struggles into sleep)
Till, leaning a lifetime to the comforter,
I float above the small limbs to their dream:

I, I, the future that mends everything.

The scenes described in the first three stanzas are peculiarly desolate—the memories of moments of childhood despondency when everything seemed paltry, disappointing, hopeless. The fourth stanza seems to counteract those memories of an unpleasant world of heat and wetness and an unattractive schoolyard and Hallowe'ens whose chief association is with rotting pumpkins and the fear of "stinking shapes of cranes and witches." The world of the fourth stanza is that of a child's aspiration toward beauty and happiness, but when read more closely the lines speak of dreams totally unrealized. "Stars beckon," and a "comforter" is imagined, but the star is "absent" in the dark world of the anxious child's nights. These images are not mere fantasy but the remembered half-nightmare feeling of a cosmic sadness in the child's mind. They are as real in the memory as "the white sun like a tin plate" and "the thin grass by the girls' door." The final ironic line, "I, I, the future that mends everything," suggests the speaker's feeling that the ultimate guilt is his own—he did not set his own adult world straight, nor did he re-create his past. He has "mended" nothing.

Jarrell's poem painfully expresses the re-experiencing of a past state of being. When this sort of thing happens—and it may be either this painful or truly ecstatic or something between these states—we are close to the subconscious realm of dreams. We may indeed actually be dreaming. Hence we may not recall the deep reverie in which, for only a second perhaps, we were lost. We may well pass through it without noticing it consciously. But we all have times when we cannot help noticing the reverie-world we have just returned from. I can remember at least two instances when I was suddenly a small child again, with sights and sounds and smells around me that I knew were precisely of the place—a particular street, or a meadow—that had returned to me in all its reality. My gratitude at those moments was indescribable. I knew then that nothing is ever finally lost to us, and that I had had similar experiences at other times but forgotten them at once. Had the return been shot with misery, as Jarrell's was, I am not sure that it would have been so delightful to feel that everything we have ever lived through remains with us always, intact.

Nevertheless, good or bad, such experiences hit us like revelations. For an eternal instant (as Proust shows so richly in *Remembrance of Things Past* that I will not allow myself to go into detail here about my own knowledge of the same thing), we are not what we are but what we once were. The sharing of memories between people intimately in touch with one another may bring a kindred "revelation." It may arouse a state of sympathy in which at least one of them "remembers" things that never happened to him, as if he were actually the other person. Yeats's poem "Among School Children" is based on sympathetic memory of this kind, memory that at first reinforces a depressed feeling he has fallen into but then leads him to try to face the feeling down directly. In this poem Yeats, who was a member of the Irish Senate, describes himself making an official visit to a girls' school. Self-consciously aware of how he must appear to the little girls, and therefore identifying himself with them for the moment, he recalls what a loved woman once told him, when they were both much younger, about an incident of her own childhood. He recalls, as well, her "Ledaean body," classically beautiful like that of Leda, whom Zeus ravished in the form of a swan, or like that of Leda's daughter Helen of Troy, born of that mating. And suddenly he remembers something that is not his to remember. But here is the passage:

> the children's eyes
> In momentary wonder stare upon
> A sixty-year-old smiling public man.
>
> I dream of a Ledaean body, bent
> Above a sinking fire, a tale that she
> Told of a harsh reproof, or trivial event
> That changed some childish day to tragedy—
> Told, and it seemed that our two natures blent
> Into a sphere from youthful sympathy,
> Or else, to alter Plato's parable,
> Into the yolk and white of the one shell.
>
> And thinking of that fit of grief or rage
> I look upon one child or t'other there
> And wonder if she stood so at that age—
> For even daughters of the swan can share
> Something of every paddler's heritage—
> And had that colour upon cheek or hair,
> And thereupon my heart is driven wild:
> She stands before me as a living child.

The acute sympathy the young lovers had felt, the night they talked near the "sinking fire," had created a mood of exalted sharing of memories. Now, in his role of esteemed public figure in the classroom, Yeats remembers his insight that night into what it had meant to be an unhappy schoolgirl. Not only does he dream back into a vision that recovers that moment of love and understanding, but all at once a second vision comes, so intense that his "heart is driven wild." It is the vision of her in school among the children before him: "She stands before me as a living child," the child she once was. Once again, as long ago, he has experienced sympathetic memory. He has "remembered" and "seen" what was not his to remember and see. The experience is almost mystical yet at the same time rooted in something very familiar, the close communion of lovers. The passage beautifully reminds us of our fierce reluctance to sacrifice what we, or even others, have known. Around these two visions the later elaborations of the poem are conceived. In fact, the incidental allusions in this passage to Plato's *Symposium* and to the folk tale of the ugly duckling, both important in the poem's development, depend for their force on these memories that explode into consciousness in the midst of the speaker's ordinary official duties.

The four poems I have just been discussing are all instances of the pressure of memory on poetic imagination under the influence of extraordinary psychic intensity. Yet the intensity I speak of can, and does, occur in every life. The man swept weeping back to the world of his boyhood by the song of a woman, the mental patient suddenly a child again and secure with his mother, the guilt-laden adult suddenly recalling bleak scenes of childhood, the elderly poet visiting the girls' school and excitedly envisioning his beloved, first as a young beauty and then as a little girl—these figures are remarkable, not as unusual persons but only because they are caught in rare but recognizable states of consciousness. They are introduced to us through the personal memories of the speakers, and are at once made part of our own memories. Memory is the key to communion, bringing people into sympathy, and art of every kind adds to the range of communion by revealing precise shadings of the experiences of others. In a very broad sense, poetry can be seen as a way of making available to our memories, through language, the private relation each person has to the world. The poems of a previous chapter added to our memories the private worlds of Sandburg's dreamy patron of the Ohio River fish shack, Frost's dirt farmer digging his potatoes (and his other farmer about to clear the pasture stream and fetch the calf), and Stevens's charmingly melancholy lady with her Sunday morning musings.

If it is valuable to realize what it is to be human—the possibilities of human feeling in action under the most varied circumstances—then poetry has this value supremely. Psychology seeks out the principles underlying the mind's action rather than the precise subjective quality of individual experience. Poetry depends absolutely on its idiosyncratic truthfulness to the poet's own sense of reality. No search for abstract theories is allowed to violate the process. We may discover all sorts of things through poetry, but the poet who has not fallen from grace can no more predict his "findings" or even "control his experiment" than a baby can predetermine its own parenthood or its own future. As a developed artist, of course, the poet is far from being a baby. He can consciously get the hang of the process he is involved with and find the right form for letting it unfold a curve of movement that answers to his need. Memory plays a tremendous role in all this. Lawrence had to catch hold of what had happened to him as he listened to the singer at her piano, had to realize how the music had evoked another time and place with another woman and different music. The "casting down" of his manhood, for instance, is a feeling that not everyone else would have had as a decisive element in this nostalgic seizure. Again, the memory of sitting under the piano, conscious of his mother's "small, poised feet," is so individual that we can be fairly sure no other poet would be likely to stress the same detail even though he might well write about a similar experience. Lawrence's choice of simple rhyming couplets and of a rather uneven metrical pattern of five-stress and six-stress lines with a good many rough variations helps him get the effect of unsubtle and spontaneous speech. As if he were writing a popular ballad, he has a trite phrase or two and some melodramatic effects. He wants to reproduce the rush of turbulent emotion leading to the breakdown of control that he experienced.

The passage by Clarke, on the other hand, emphasizes the drop from violent sensations in the preceding stanza to an atmosphere of sleepy stillness, uneventful except as seen from the vantage point of a bitterly disturbed mental condition. From that vantage point, it seems unutterably desirable: everything comforting, unchallenging, under control. Clarke's lines are compressed, with no regular rhyme scheme but with a tight four-stress line and many subtly interlinked sounds that establish the secure childhood world the patient remembers. Notice for instance that almost all the words beginning with *s* evoke that world: "smaller," "seven," "sleep," "secret." The apparent exceptions are "soon" and "sewing." But "soon" introduces the first line and shares in its tone of suggesting a magical tale for children: "Soon Mnemosyne had made him smaller." And "sewing" is associated with the mother's reassuring presence—

> at her sewing machine,
> The shuttle clicking as she followed
> A hem . . .

Clarke, an unusually artful manipulator of sound, fills the stanza with words humming with quiet activity, all connected by their *ing* endings as the other words were by their initial *s*'s: "sewing," "clicking," "praying," "hiding." Again, by putting "elder-trees" and "elders" in succeeding lines he gently links the human and natural worlds. Without wanting to over-complicate my discussion, I should note that the language in which he suggests his hero's momentary recovery of a happy child's secure little world may have its negative side— an undercurrent of fear of the sinister outside forces threatening that world. The grown-up world of work is present too, darkness is coming on, words like "hiding" and "secret" might foreshadow later terror, and even the description of the mother with her sewing machine and its clicking shuttle may suggest the Fates. But the primary effect is of an idyllic atmosphere within the normal range of life, which does include (without our paying it much heed ordinarily) life's dangers. That atmosphere is broken with a jolt in Clarke's next stanza, where the paranoid hallucinations of the hero return without warning:

> Suddenly over the lower wall,
> Madmen were leaping into the yard
> With howls of "Murder!"

So the instant of calm rediscovery of childhood is past. We are back where loss and madness reign. Between this point and the ending, the poem still has much ground to cover before the hero is allowed to re-enter the world that has all but destroyed him. At the end, still alienated but with his memory restored, he returns to modern, commercialized, lost Dublin in what must be one of the more depressed "happy endings" in poetry:

> Upon that site
> Of shares and dividends in sight
> Of Watling Street and the Cornmarket,
> At Number One in Thomas Street
> Shone in the days of the ballad-sheet,
> The house in which his mother was born.

Yeats's "Among School Children" deals with shocks of recognition through memory just as Lawrence's and Clarke's poems do; but it presents neither a temporary breakdown of adult identity like Lawrence's nor a morbid psychological crisis like Clarke's. The depression it struggles against is common to aging people. Aware of how children must see him, the poet feels a stab of chagrin at the image of himself as "a sixty-year-old smiling public man." The feeling stirs up a passionate memory of that earlier time when he was young and he and his love shared a thrill of perfect sympathy. Then he remembers how they both have changed, and soon he is plunged into some very painful thoughts. These center on the differences between a young mother's dreams and the "scarecrow" her baby must eventually become in old age, and between *all* human dreams or ideals and life's realities. Finally, in a transport of reaction against despair, he asserts that in creative action we do reach a state beyond the touch of disillusionment and decay. There labor "blossoms" in such a way that the real and the ideal become one:

Labour is blossoming or dancing where
The body is not bruised to pleasure soul,
Nor beauty born out of its own despair,
Nor blear-eyed wisdom out of midnight oil.
O chestnut-tree, great rooted blossomer,
Are you the leaf, the blossom or the bole?
O body swayed to music, O brightening glance,
How can we know the dancer from the dance?

"Among School Children," then, begins with a startling vision in the classroom but becomes an exploration of the self-disillusionment of old age and the essential triumph over it that creative reaction rooted in intense vision can bring. The progress of this meditative poem is a little like that of Stevens's "Sunday Morning"; strongly projected scenes and images give clarity and excitement and the depth of real experience to a line of thought that is sometimes very simple and sometimes elusive. The delightful lady of "Sunday Morning" felt sad when she thought about death. The excitable poet of "Among School Children" gets into an internal frenzy (we may be sure he shows no sign of it to the children or to "the kind old nun" who is showing him through the convent school) thinking of a similar subject: growing old. The greater power of Yeats's poem comes in part from its greater concentration, and this in turn derives from the speaker's fierce contemplation of his present self in relation to his passionate memories. He gathers his thoughts and images around him for a leap into the assertion that there *is* a place in the life of the mind that transcends the working of time and fate. The blazing pictures that came into his mind in the lines I have quoted have already shown that this place is the point at which significant memory touches the active imagination.

For the reader who starts with the actual starting point of Yeats's poem, the simplicity and naturalness of the way the poem moves must be evident. The original situation, the memories, the ideas about aging and disillusionment are so normal as to be plain. What is not plain or commonplace is the powerful phrasing, in which the poet's aroused intelligence makes itself felt. His eight-line stanza with its simple yet varied rhyme scheme and its five-stress lines—the *ottava rima* Yeats loved to use—allows a skilled poet enough room and flexibility so that he can develop his ideas and vary his tones and his intensity at the same time. Lawrence, Clarke, and Jarrell use less demanding forms. The rhyming couplets, rough rhythms, and sweeping, occasionally trite diction of "Piano" are sufficient for this poem, which is almost a psychological ballad; that is, it is a simple narrative in bold broad strokes about an experience that is largely inward and passive. The shorter lines and complex inner structure and suggestiveness of both *Mnemosyne Lay in Dust* and "The Elementary Scene" are suitable for conveying a subtle awareness. Yeats's stanza form and range of vocabulary allow him to create either sort of effect as well as to give free rein to a mind racing to press the meaning of his classroom experience to its limits.

Another poem of his, "Demon and Beast," starts from forgetting rather than from memory. It has to do with something that happens in old age when the daily pressures that define our conscious daily lives fall away—a state that we might conceivably call senility were it not that the poem is so magnificently articulate and intelligently thought out at the same time. Moreover, the condition the poem is describing is so unselfconscious that an effort of memory, after all, is necessary to recall it later on and to suggest its character to the reader. The mood, the directness, are quite natural; although the ideas are not commonplace, the situation around which they grow could be that of anyone. As in "Among School Children," the essential basis of the poem is a straightforward reaction to an ordinary human situation. The speaker has been overcome with a sense of bliss. In the climactic stanza he realizes its amazing source—the weakness of old age, which in other poems Yeats bitterly resents. "I am certain," he declares,

> that mere growing old, that brings
> Chilled blood, that sweetness brought;
> Yet have no dearer thought
> Than that I might find out a way
> To make it linger half a day.

"Demon and Beast" is a poem about the joy of release from passionate involvement with life, not through an act of will but because the body fails. The speaker has seen himself experiencing something like senile ecstasy. It is a condition hard to describe, something both obvious and elusive. The first stanza introduces the theme mysteriously but grows simple at the end:

> For certain minutes at the least
> That crafty demon and that loud beast
> That plague me day and night
> Ran out of my sight;
> Though I had long perned in the gyre,
> Between my hatred and desire,
> I saw my freedom won
> And all laugh in the sun.

At the full of life we are driven by powerful needs and tensions within our personalities. The speaker thinks of this condition as being "plagued" by his hatreds and his desires— "perning in a gyre" between them (that is, being whirled between them in a constant spiraling movement that brings him now closer to his spiritual and intellectual "demon," now to his body's "loud beast"). But these forces had receded "for certain minutes at the least" and left him free for joy. The next stanza tells us that even certain portraits in Dublin's National Gallery, one of them a "death's head" and another the face of a grim conspirator, had "said Welcome" to him and "smiled" and "beckoned to sweet company." It was as if they had been welcoming him into their realm beyond life, where differences of ideology, morality, faith, and personality no longer matter. It seems, in one sense, a preparation for death, a promise that death will release us from all life's torments without our *really* dying. If one is brought into this state of feeling, as Yeats tells us he was, then the result is something far more positive than happy senility: a reopening of oneself to the world of primal experience.

> But soon a tear-drop started up,
> For aimless joy had made me stop
> Beside the little lake
> To watch a white gull take
> A bit of bread thrown up into the air;
> Now gyring here and there
> He splashed where an absurd
> Portly green-pated bird
> Shook off the water from his back;
> Being no more demoniac
> A stupid happy creature
> Could rouse my whole nature.

This stanza, whose scene is St. Stephen's Green, not far from Dublin's National Gallery, is a delightful example of Yeats's art. The rhyming couplets, with lines of unequal length and a sprinkling of off-rhymes, convey both the speaker's sense of blessed release and joy and his thoughtful observation of his own state. To recapture the experience whole, Yeats has to catch the most elementary details that entered into the mood together with the exact quality of the mood. What appears so simple is in fact a powerful stroke of memory, memory of the living quality of an experience that in part was not a conscious experience. The rhyming comes as a series of singing couplets that chant the speaker's remembered ecstasy—very different from the more involved stanzas of "Among School Children." At the same time, the off-rhymes and shifting lengths suggest the mind going over the meaning of what it has experienced. In the same way, the language of the passage is studded with boldly naive, plain, concrete words (often monosyllables) and phrases: "tear-drop," "little lake," "white gull," "a bit of bread," "portly green-pated

bird"; but the effect is somewhat modified, made more sophisticated, by the abstract phrase "aimless joy," the almost arcane
"gyring" and "perning," the detached adjective "absurd," and
the engaging but philosophical three lines at the end.

From here the poem takes us to its climactic stanza—with
the passage quoted earlier that recognizes the cause of this
ecstasy: "mere growing old, that brings/ Chilled blood." The
final stanza then shifts our attention to a quite esoteric set of
references, literally far away in both time and space from the
homely world of gulls and ducks and relaxed citizens in St.
Stephen's Green. The poem now speaks of "barren Thebaid"
and "the Mareotic Sea"—that is, of the region associated with
fourth-century Christian monasticism in Egypt—and of "exultant Anthony," the saint who was its founder. These ascet-
ics renounced worldly power and passions and let themselves
starve. Yeats imagines that as they grew weaker they discovered an ecstasy they no longer needed to will, for their sheer
weakness brought it to them:

> O what a sweetness strayed
> Through barren Thebaid
> Or by the Mareotic Sea
> When that exultant Anthony
> And twice a thousand more
> Starved upon the shore
> And withered to a bag of bones!
> What had the Caesars but their thrones?

That "sweetness" was like the speaker's, experienced in the
Dublin park. In their case the paradox is even greater, though.
Not only did Anthony's followers know a pleasure that any
voluptuary would find enviable; they also, since they chose
their destiny, won a privilege beyond what the active world
can offer, one that made the power of emperors seem paltry.
Here Yeats speaks intimately of a knowledge that comes to all
of us, particularly if the thought of death or of some great
disappointment crosses our minds: the arbitrariness of our de-

sires and values. Each life has its own peculiar demon and beast—very well. But there are times when we glimpse the exquisite release we might feel without them, if only we were no longer driven to seek out sensual or psychological or even spiritual gratification. Perhaps we are dealing here with what Freud calls the death wish. Though few of us would dare exchange the known satisfactions of life for the negative, unpredictable ecstasy of "chilled blood" and dying into "a bag of bones," the vision of that possible ecstasy holds deep and clear in the psyche. It is associated with the release of falling asleep and of every kind of pleasurable self-oblivion.

"Demon and Beast," then, is built around Yeats's memory of a single point of experience that endured "for certain moments at the least." Those moments might have come and gone unnoted—like the memories in Lawrence's and Clarke's poems and in Yeats's "Among School Children," salvaged from the subconscious life by the pressure of circumstance. To hold those moments in view, however, is for the speaker in "Demon and Beast" to sustain a pitch of memory that includes other elusive tones of awareness too: the demon and beast constantly driving him, his animistic feeling of the independent life of the portraits in the National Gallery, and his fascination with the mode of life sought out by Anthony and his followers—so alien to his own existence. The sweetness into which he sank has become not only a negatively blissful condition but an energizing and organizing source both for his memory and for his intellectual and historical interests. It has led him to remember the precise quality of a precious and disappearing experience and has brought diverse interests and feelings into focus as a single fused realization. The poem gives a brilliant impression of a thoughtful, learned person deeply engaged with a sensation of a complex sort. There is the basic, almost primitively mystical onset of childlike joy. But at the same time, we see the knowledgeable range of consciousness of a mature and cultivated man being brought under the influence of this primal state.

That is perhaps the greatest delight of the poem, especially in the final stanza when what would ordinarily be dry, specialized historical knowledge is transformed through the ecstatic outburst with which the stanza begins. The transport of joy has brought him closer to his ordinary life and mind than before. He sees himself up close—accepting his old age, seeing the portraits as alive (they might seem *frighteningly* alive if he were in a slightly different mood), standing in St. Stephen's Green, and thinking about mysticism and asceticism. The speaker has made himself all the more real to us through his outburst of ecstatic memory.

Musics of Awareness: Time and Space

Yeats's "Demon and Beast," we have just seen, is a rather complex poem that discovers something exceedingly simple. The speaker's more sophisticated self drops away, and what is left is pure delight in the realities all around him. True enough, he then puts all his passion, learning, and intelligence to work trying to understand what has happened. But the special music of "Demon and Beast" comes from the fresh, naive joy that overwhelms him "for certain minutes at the least." The music of our elementary awareness, joyous or not, accompanies us always.

This music of awareness, coming from the impact of both the external world and our own inward psychic and physical states, is one of the most common sources of poetry. It is really inseparable from being a human being and existing within time and space. That situation can never be entirely static, for even if we ourselves are not in motion our senses are generally alert to whatever comes their way. And when we *are* in motion that fact in itself becomes an important element in our awareness. A child, for instance, becomes aware of itself as a small running or swimming or skating creature. A man or woman driving a car on a highway becomes aware of the changing landscape as a flowing series of impressions; these merge into one another at a certain pace, with certain expected repetitions and certain variations. These common sorts of experience are like listening to music, if one's consciousness is at all keyed up, or if the motion itself has created a deep reverie attuned to it.

Many poems arise from a poet's catching his awareness in motion and feeling its rhythmic pulsation at the same time. My poem "Geometries of Manhattan: Morning" provides a simple example. In it a music of reverie accompanies the motion of the eye. The speaker is relatively still; as he looks out over Manhattan from a hotel window, his eye moves toward the western horizon and back, and his thoughts and feelings move with it. When something blocks his vision, there is a balked effect both in the rhythm and the thought; where the eyesweep is unhindered, at least in imagination, the lines grow longer and there are fewer stop sounds and punctuation breaks. The sense of a concentrated vision, not altogether happy, at the end is related to a different kind of motion of the eye as it follows an object falling through the air.

Foggy morning, The mist-held horizons
move closer, being broken now
by hulks without grace or thrust, not skyscrapers,
not experiments—dumped crates, deadweights
dropped by monsters on strike against the sun.
They block a mile of river, mile of sky.

                          Still stately, serene,
the thwarted Hudson poises them in its frame
while weary, soiled, the massed clouds brace them. The aching
    eye
presses, past clouds and water, to the ruined Jersey shore whose
mysterious, unfocused distances alone sustain
lost promises as mute as Leonardo's far-off forest-green.

                                  And now
the relenting eye returns, the river brightens. One gull, two,
invite the dreamer back toward the wakening city. A raindrop-
    pool
ripples on a factory rooftop. A tiny cardboard carton

> drifts from some crevice in the glittering heights,
> a box-kite to the lucky watcher. Turning, turning,
> past this hotel window, downward to older Manhattan
> drifting and turning, towards the unseeing multitudes, the cars,
> the shadows, the shafts of sunlight, the life below.

The eye meets interference in the first stanza, strains to reach the farthest horizon in the second, and returns over a number of quicker, gayer points of magnetic attraction in the third until the drifting, turning carton directs it downward toward the vast, encompassing life of the people in the city below.

In an entirely different city-setting, Paul Blackburn's poem "The Once-Over" gives us a jaunty, bumpy, sexy instance of the eye's movement in space:

> The tanned blond
>   in the green print sack
> in the center of the subway car
>   standing
> tho there are seats
>   has had it from
> 1 teen-age hood
> 1 lesbian
> 1 envious housewife
> 4 men over fifty
> (& myself), in short
>   the contents of this half of the car
>
>
> Our notations are:
> long legs, long waist, high breasts (no bra), long
> neck, the model slump
>   the handbag drape & how the skirt
> cuts in under a very handsome
>   set of cheeks
> 'stirring dull roots with spring rain' sayeth the preacher
>
>   Only a stolid young man
>   with a blue business suit and the New York Times
>   does not know he is being assaulted

So.
She has us and we her
all the way to downtown Brooklyn
Over the tunnel and through the bridge
                    to DeKalb Avenue we go
  all very chummy

She stares at the number over the door
                    and gives no sign
  Yet the sign is on her

   This poem, an animated caricature in words, nevertheless
reports one kind of heightening of ordinary consciousness.
The scene is presented as comic on the surface, yet finally is
by no means completely so. Consider the situation. The subway car is rushing through space, mostly in the dark, and so
we have an isolated scene in motion. The blonde young
woman has stationed herself at the center of the scene, vivid
in her green dress and fleshly presence. It is with her, amid
the converging designs of both the train's and the eye's mo-
tions, that the speaker begins. The rhythms, marked both by
the line breaks and by the indentations, reflect the way his
eye shifts and the way the train lurches as it goes forward.
The poet points us first to the young woman's place in the
subway car and then to a catalogue of her willingly captive
audience. He projects himself as part of it; and it is interesting
that, though he modestly puts "and myself" in parentheses, he
has reserved for himself the position of emphasis at the end of
the catalogue. It is his heightened awareness, after all, that defines the situation and the pacing of attention here. The way
he identifies the other people—the "hood," the "lesbian," the
"housewife," the "4 men over fifty"—and tells us their
thoughts is of course the working of his own imagination.
   The poem's movement, then, is that of the speaker's awareness and imagination. It is he—"myself"—who speaks for the
whole little community of "this half of the car," and it is his
voice that guides us straight back to the image in all their
eyes: the young woman in the middle. A second catalogue

follows, this time of her charms. It is lustfully and sardoni-
cally appreciative, and the quotation from T. S. Eliot's *The
Waste Land* (" 'stirring dull roots with spring rain' sayeth the
preacher") that concludes it neatly suggests the kind of be-
musement she has stirred up in her temporary companions.
Only one belatedly noticed young man sits, imperviously
bourgeois, a solid, stolid block of sculpture, in his little separate stanza set off to the right. It takes a small eye-lurch to
move to that stanza, which interrupts the music of the continuous erotic circuit that begins and ends with the "tanned
blond." But then we look back at the main scene again, the
little, sexually hypnotized group riding together, and the poem
pitches into a jolly rhythm that parodies "Over the river and
through the trees." At the very end, though, the tone under-
goes a change. The speaker is suddenly serious, mystical.
Though his phrasing is still a bit playful, he brings out the
sense of a "sign" given and understood, a covenant offered but
not fully entered into. A modern Venus has appeared from
nowhere. She has enchanted and aroused a half-dozen people.
After giving them a revelation of beauty that neither they nor
she can quite understand or deal with, she—like them—will
disappear back into the ordinary life.

Blackburn's poem is certainly rooted in that life; his scene
has all the ingredients that make up everyday New York reality of a certain kind. What makes the poem (as distinct
from the scene) extraordinary is the way the speaker catches
his own thought in action and relates it to what he sees by
making it all a controlled, shifting music of awareness. Probably the average man on that subway car would notice the
same things about the subway Venus that Blackburn's speaker
notices. He would feel the same half-comic transport of desire and appreciation, and he would be left with a kindred
feeling of a promise not quite realized. He might or might not
—this average man—be so keenly aware of the other people
present and of the ironies of the situation. The thing least
likely to occur to his conscious mind would be the fact that

he was taking part in a rhythmic, dramatic, or dance scene, yet even this fact would be present, like the sense of loss, deep in his subconscious mind. Blackburn's poem is great fun, a joyous holding of the experience by means of language. But it touches depths that are not at all trivial. Indeed, Blackburn, whose translations of the medieval Provençal troubadours are among the finest yet done, gives a typically high-spirited description of a desirable lady, such as the troubadours often wrote, in his second stanza ("long legs, long waist . . ."), but with some necessarily modern touches. And the note of a mystery somehow frustrated in its unfolding with which "The Once-Over" ends is not far from the plaintive note of many a medieval love song. In Blackburn's translations from the poems of Peire Vidal (1175-1205), for instance, we find the question:

> But why does she signal and welcome me so gently
>   if she has no intention
> of granting me what the lack of which so pains me?

This is exactly the feeling, after all the boisterous preparation for unrealized ecstasy is over, with which Blackburn's own poem ends—and which, for that matter, baffles all men and women to some extent, again and again. Like the "she" of Peire Vidal's lines, the girl in the subway car "gives no sign" although "the sign is on her"—she both signals and withholds herself.

Blackburn's preoccupation in these poems reminds me of a passage in William Carlos Williams's long sequence *Paterson*, one of the great modern explorations of the poetry implicit in the common life all around us. In *Paterson* Williams tries to search out the right language and rhythmic forms to express the daily experience, the history, the frustrations, and the potentialities of the people in an industrial American city. Like Blackburn's "The Once-Over," the passage I am thinking of reports and comments on a casual encounter—this time among the crowds on a city street.

There is a woman in our town
walks rapidly, flat bellied
in worn slacks upon the street
where I saw her.
                          neither short
nor tall, nor old nor young
her
          face would attract no

adolescent. Grey eyes looked
straight before her.
                          Her
                                   hair
was gathered simply behind the
ears under a shapeless hat.

Her
          hips were narrow, her
                                        legs
thin and straight. She stopped
me in my tracks—until I saw
her
          disappear in the crowd.

An inconspicuous decoration
made of sombre cloth, meant
I think to be a flower, was
pinned flat to her
                          right

breast—any woman might have
done the same to
say she was a woman and warn
us of her mood. Otherwise

she was dressed in male attire,
as much as to say to hell
with you. Her
                          expression was
serious, her
                    feet were small.

And she was gone!

if ever I see you again
as I have sought you
daily without success

I'll speak to you, alas
too late! ask,
What are you doing on the

streets of Paterson? a
thousand questions:
Are you married? Have you any

children? And, most important,
your NAME! which
of course she may not

give me—though
I cannot conceive it
in such a lonely and

intelligent woman

have you read anything that I have written?
It is all for you . . .

This "woman in our town" is no creature of male sexual fantasy suddenly come to life. She is "flat bellied." Her face would "attract no adolescent"—an observation that discounts her beauty only in the most ironic way. She *is* a woman, she does have breasts; the "inconspicuous decoration" she wears calls subtle attention to these facts. But she will not permit herself to be viewed frivolously, as attested by her "sombre cloth" and "male attire" and "serious" expression (despite her "small" feet—a quick, appreciative notation of her femininity the poet cannot help making). She does not parade herself like Blackburn's subway blonde. Yet she too grips the speaker's excited imagination. The "sign is on her" just as surely— *more* surely. This passage is the only time we meet her in *Paterson*, but the poet says that everything he has ever written has been for her. He thus makes her out to be very important indeed. *Paterson* as a whole is concerned with what the poet considers the absence of a "common language" in America. A destructive, divisive tendency in the country, he thinks, blocks off communication and encourages impersonal violence. One would have to read the rest of *Paterson* to see that the way the woman appears and disappears on the crowded street symbolizes the important shared meanings of our civilization that keep eluding us.

These ideas are basic themes of *Paterson*, and because of them it is important that this woman neither denies nor exploits her sexuality. She is a figure of common humanity, its feminine side, and—says the poet—"she stopped me in my tracks." No wonder. Her devastating effect is in part because, in the midst of ordinary life, he has seen his Muse, a democratic, working-class Muse of the modern age. What he has seen is like Whitman's vision, over a century ago in *Song of Myself:* "I am the mate and companion of people, all just as immortal and fathomless as myself." The vision is not in some sacred grotto or magic isle but—to quote Whitman again—on the city street amid

> The blab of the pave, tires of carts, sluff of boot-soles,
>   talk of the promenaders,
> The heavy omnibus, the driver with his interrogating
>   thumb, the clank of the shod horses . . .

We should have to substitute automobiles for horses, but otherwise this could be the very scene in which Williams finds his Muse in Paterson, New Jersey. His poem is epic in its intention and scope, and readers of Homer's *Odyssey* may see in the description of the woman's "grey eyes" and in the emphasis on her intelligence an allusion to Athene, the goddess who guided Odysseus through his epic trials. Of all the women characters that appear in *Paterson*, this figure most memorably concentrates meanings our world has all but forgotten how to understand and respond to. Muse, goddess, apparition, real woman glimpsed for an unforgettable instant, she is all the women of the poem in one—the ideal figure for whom and to whom the poet's awakened mind speaks.

But let us return to the passage itself, so much clearer and more direct and rhythmically alive than anything one can say about it in mere prose. The impression the woman makes is a swift one. She "walks rapidly" into a sort of motion-picture closeup, and all the subdued details of her appearance become bold and even striking as she comes into focus. The speaker pauses, stunned. Then he notices subtler details of her dress and expression, and "she was gone!" The exclamation echoes the earlier effect of "She stopped/ me in my tracks." And now, in her absence, a new tone of passionate address and questioning is introduced.

These are visual and emotional shifts as the whole experience is gathered in and then recedes. Meanwhile, the music of the passage is like what the poet says about the woman: quiet, apparently muted, yet in reality full of charged, dynamic effects. The first lines are deliberately flat and a bit hurried and stumbling. Then, beginning with "Neither short/ nor tall," a chanting and balanced music takes over. Between lines four and twenty, we are guided in our pacing, pauses, and interpretation of the sound stresses by the repetition of the words "her" and "nor"; by the repeated h's, especially in "her," "hair," "hat," "hips," and "hell"; and by the repeated n's of "neither," "nor," "no," and "narrow." Later, the words "I" and "you" become particularly important. Without going into more detail, let me suggest that the reader who speaks the poem aloud, pausing momentarily to stress each of these repeated words and sounds as he does so and also pausing for the fraction of a second at the end of each line, will be able to catch the precise way that Williams makes an exquisite melody out of very plain and natural speech. The music of his vision, and then of his longing to recapture it, is inseparable from the feeling that here, before our eyes and in the most everyday places, lies the clue to everything in life we cherish and want to encourage.

How does a poet come to write a passage like this one, or a poem like "The Once-Over" or "Geometries of Manhattan:

Morning"? The essential answer is that, being a poet, he seeks out the right language and form for getting at the heart of a real or imagined experience. Perhaps "seeks out" sounds too deliberate, though, for in practice a poem usually begins as a phrase or line that echoes some feeling not yet altogether clear—an almost instinctive impulse of language in search of whatever it was that got it started. Poets or not, we all go through the process of absorbing an experience, becoming more or less conscious of its importance to us, and letting our minds and imaginations play over it. Because the process is natural, human, and common to all people, it is particularly satisfying to the poet when a turn of speech, with its own innate rhythm, comes into his head and holds the literal memory and flavor of the experience. Colloquialisms like "She stopped me in my tracks" and "as much as to say to hell with you" came right out of the air, so to speak, and into Williams's poem. That is half the art, just to bring in the right language, colloquial or formal, that shimmers around the memory of an experience and defines it, just as light and shadow and color define some object caught by the eye and held in focus.

The other half of the art, of course, is to *make* something with the language—once the language itself has pointed the way. Many people are alive to language, but the poet needs to create with it a pure design of insight and emotion and thus give human dimension to the raw stuff of existence. That is where the formally elegant and traditional side of any art comes into its own. I have thought, seeing the intricately satisfying designs woven into Touareg tent walls, how those designs made an infinitely expanding world out of what would otherwise have been the narrow, stifling confines of the primitive tents of desert nomads. Every art does the same. It expresses what we feel and experience but also weaves a pattern of human design and meaning out of the threads and colors of reality. By the imaginative and skillful use of form it frees us from our ordinary limits, which are not our real limits once the mind's power to project itself is freed.

So the simple, sensuous response to reality as we move through time and space, or even as we stand receiving the touch of that reality through all our senses, is both the source of the poet's special excitement of language and his seismograph. By it he gauges the intensities of the world around him and the means he will use to deal with them. The superbly confident lines near the beginning of Whitman's *Song of Myself* that assert his relation to literal reality are a fine statement of how the poet feels all this. These lines refer as well to the most elementary bases of music and rhythm in the working of the human body: heartbeat, breathing, making love, and the longer cycles of sleeping and waking. Although our conscious minds are alert to most of these rhythms only in special circumstances, our subconscious minds at least are always intricately responsive to them. When all is well—as in Whitman's poem—an exuberant gaiety marks our awareness of the whole life rhythm:

Houses and rooms are full of perfumes, the shelves are
    crowded with perfumes,
I breathe the fragrance myself and know and like it,
The distillation would intoxicate me also, but I shall
    not let it.

The atmosphere is not a perfume, it has no taste of the
    distillation, it is odorless,
It is for my mouth forever, I am in love with it,
I will go to the bank by the wood and become undisguised
    and naked.
I am mad for it to be in contact with me.

The smoke of my own breath,
Echoes, ripples, buzz'd whispers, love-root, silk-thread,
    crotch and vine,
My respiration and inspiration, the beating of my heart,
    the passing of blood and air through my lungs,
The sniff of green leaves and dry leaves, and of the shore
    and dark-color'd sea-rocks, and of hay in the barn,

The sound of the belch'd words of my voice loos'd to the
    eddies of the wind,

A few light kisses, a few embraces, a reaching around of
    arms,
The play of shine and shade on the trees as the supple
    boughs wag,
The delight alone or in the rush of the streets, or along
    the fields and hill-sides,
The feeling of health, the full-noon trill, the song of me
    rising from bed and meeting the sun.

Have you reckon'd a thousand acres much? have you reckon'd
    the earth much?
Have you practis'd so long to learn to read?
Have you felt so proud to get at the meaning of poems?

Stop this day and night with me and you shall possess the
    origin of all poems,
You shall possess the good of the earth and sun, (there are
    millions of suns left,)
You shall no longer take things at second or third hand,
    nor look through the eyes of the dead, nor feed on the
    spectres in books,
You shall not look through my eyes either, nor take things
    from me,
You shall listen to all sides and filter them from your self.

We may want to cry out, "*Walt*, do you really want to say
'*belch'd* words'? Do the boughs really '*wag*'?" But, taken as
a whole, the passage is a perfect indication of the continuous
interplay of the poet's senses and his active intelligence. The
sensuous apprehension is of the poet's own bodily processes
as well as of the world outside him. He doesn't wish to "distil"
fragrant essences; he wishes to get life down as it is, on the
run, and then send it forth again so that his readers can have
it whole to absorb into themselves and to reconceive in their
own ways.

I have digressed a little from my strict theme in this chapter. I wanted to show the connection between that theme—
the music of awareness within time and space—and the way
poems actually begin to make themselves. Now I want to turn
to a passage that illustrates my theme more fully than any I

have yet quoted, involving as it does a sustained action on the part of the speaker. It has a high seriousness that helps it re-create a remembered time as beautifully as any poem I have ever read. The passage comes near the beginning of Words-worth's long autobiographical poem, *The Prelude*, written and revised between 1798 and 1839. It is an account of a ter-rifying childhood experience that left the deepest kind of im-pression on Wordsworth's mind. But let me delay looking at it for a brief moment. Just before this point in *The Prelude*, Wordsworth has been meditating thankfully on the mysteri-ous process by which Nature makes an organic whole of all the elements, sweet and bitter, of our lives. One could argue that, in a much more abstract way, his prayerful praise of life here is not finally unlike Whitman's sensuous paean to life in the lines from *Song of Myself* just cited. But Wordsworth's meditation is eloquently rhetorical and analytical:

> Dust as we are, the immortal spirit grows
> Like harmony in music; there is a dark
> Inscrutable workmanship that reconciles
> Discordant elements, makes them cling together
> In one society. How strange that all
> The terrors, pains, and early miseries,
> Regrets, vexations, lassitudes interfused
> Within my mind, should e'er have borne a part,
> And that a needful part, in making up
> The calm existence that is mine when I
> Am worthy of myself! Praise to the end!
> Thanks to the means which Nature deigned to employ;
> Whether her fearless visitings, or those
> That came with soft alarm, like hurtless light
> Opening the peaceful clouds; or she may use
> Severer interventions, ministry
> More palpable, as best might suit her aim.

After this stanza (to which I shall return), Wordsworth gives us the terrifying account I have mentioned. He presents it as an example of Nature's "severer interventions" that for-cibly affect the character of a growing child. I have quoted the preceding stanza because it is intended to introduce this account, and also because of the striking change between its style and the absolutely direct, energetic style of the longer passage that follows. In the longer passage, surface details emerge sharply, all seen from the viewpoint of the boy who has stolen a boat and begun to row it over a silent lake under the stars and a brilliant moon. The moonlight is reflected in the water and seems to converge on him during all the moments of gathering excitement as he moves through a constantly changing scene. The only abstractions in the passage are the word "her" (referring to Nature) in the first line, the phrases that describe the boy's feeling of guilt ("act of stealth," "troubled pleasure"), the enormously impressive line "As if with voluntary power instinct" (to suggest the shock of seeing a huge peak suddenly emerge from among the hills and seem to stride after him), and some of the phrases evoking the aftermath of depression toward the end.

> One summer evening (led by her) I found
> A little boat tied to a willow tree
> Within a rocky cave, its usual home.
> Straight I unloosed her chain, and stepping in
> Pushed from the shore. It was an act of stealth
> And troubled pleasure, nor without the voice
> Of mountain-echoes did my boat move on;
> Leaving behind her still, on either side,
> Small circles glittering idly in the moon,
> Until they melted all into one track
> Of sparkling light. But now, like one who rows,
> Proud of his skills, to reach a chosen point
> With an unswerving line, I fixed my view
> Upon the summit of a craggy ridge,
> The horizon's utmost boundary; for above
> Was nothing but the stars and the grey sky.
> She was an elfin pinnace; lustily
> I dipped my oars into the silent lake,
> And, as I rose upon the stroke, my boat
> Went heaving through the water like a swan;
> When, from behind that craggy steep till then
> The horizon's bound, a huge peak, black and huge,

As if with voluntary power instinct
Upreared its head. I struck and struck again,
And growing still in stature the grim shape
Towered up between me and the stars, and still,
For so it seemed, with purpose of its own
And measured motion like a living thing,
Strode after me. With trembling oars I turned,
And through the silent water stole my way
Back to the covert of the willow tree;
There in her mooring-place I left my bark,—
And through the meadows homeward went, in grave
And serious mood; but after I had seen
That spectacle, for many days, my brain
Worked with a dim and undetermined sense
Of unknown modes of being; o'er my thoughts
There hung a darkness, call it solitude
Or blank desertion. No familiar shapes
Remained, no pleasant images of trees,
Of sea or sky, no colours of green fields;
But huge and mighty forms, that do not live
Like living men, moved slowly through the mind
By day, and were a trouble to my dreams.

This long stanza is one of the truly remarkable narrative passages in English poetry. The events and effects described have the ring of accuracy in every physical detail, yet the experience is essentially a moral one at the same time. The boy's hasty, furtive use of a boat not his own for a row on the lake begins in a mood of guilty decisiveness, almost as though he had planned to test his own ability to enjoy himself despite a well-developed conscience. That mood is replaced—or at any rate repressed—by the sheer exhilaration of what he is doing, until the huge peak appears, the very embodiment of moral vengeance in the boy's eyes, and turns the glorious triumphant effort when he had the boat "heaving through the water like a swan" into a hideous escapade.

Underlying this moral and psychological sequence of tones and moods is the series of physical impressions that makes the passage so brilliantly alive. I don't wish to point out the obvious in something so very clearly written, but it is part of the experience of this poem to see it in terms of that series and its impact on us as we read along. First there is the closeup of the boy finding the boat and taking it—a sort of Tom Sawyer effect. Narrowly concentrated on his actions and feelings, these lines induce us to identify ourselves with his frame of mind. But once he pushes off, the impersonal elements of the scene begin to come into their own. Mountain echoes, moonlight on the water, the great "track of sparkling light"—all these, despite certain other implications I shall soon suggest, make an atmosphere of strange and exciting beauty. The boy responds with his supreme and joyous effort. When he reaches a certain point, the great black peak appears that makes him keep up his violent rowing, but now the whole spirit of the rowing has been changed—and the peak seems to cut him off from the stars that have been part of his inspiration.

At the same time the poem's movement is ambiguous too. That is, more than one meaning is suggested, for indeed the boy's motives and responses to what he is going through are themselves ambiguous. From the start, the scene is eerie and overwhelming. The boy is isolated in his stolen little boat amid the grand solitudes of the natural world. The mountain has a "voice"; he is under a kind of void—"nothing but the stars and the grey sky"—with the moon apparently behind him, over the bow; even the boat has something supernatural, "elfin," about it; and then the "huge peak" seems diabolically conscious, "with voluntary power instinct." As these effects accumulate, making the lovely landscape appear consciously baleful, the terror of the black peak takes on nightmare proportions. Its full horror requires almost eight lines to develop. The passage ends with the boy's return of the boat and his prolonged depression after the experience is over.

The poems quoted earlier in this chapter have a glow of arousal to the possibilities for life and beauty, eroded but still vitally present, in the midst of the modern city. The arousal here is more manysided. The boy is aroused to the thrilling and beautiful mystery of Nature and at the same time to her alien, threatening power and to the monstrous visions lurking in his own soul. If the scenes the American poets describe are familiar, so is the childhood trauma Wordsworth writes about. It is interesting that, in all these poems except Whitman's, the emotion develops within a specified scope of space and time that involves changing perspectives. Wordsworth's lines, though, are by far the most dramatically conceived and concentrated. The movement of feeling in them is more dynamically arranged. The passage builds into its climax of panic followed by crushing spiritual darkness, the "blank desertion" of what seems utter defeat.

The position the boy has maneuvered himself into is not all his own doing. Wordsworth himself says, in the first line, that he had been "led by her"—that is, by Nature. Like the hero of Austin Clarke's *Mnemosyne Lay in Dust* (discussed in the last chapter), he has been cut off from his sense of himself and his past for the time being. His natural surroundings have suddenly taken on their own angry life and closed in on him. The entire atmosphere develops with a subtlety matching that of the mind's own mechanisms. Take for instance the description of the ripples left by the boat on the moonlit water:

> Leaving behind her still, on either side,
> Small circles glittering idly in the moon,
> Until they melted all into one track
> Of sparkling light. . . .

This is beautiful, precise description. Yet, in view of the uneasy atmosphere at the beginning of the boy's adventure, and the demonic presence that will dominate the poem a few lines afterwards, it is very easy to see this description as a blending of beauty and terror, at once enchanting and chilling. The ripples make small circles of reflected moonlight, but just saying that they are *in* the moon suggests a displacement of our sense of the natural order. The word "idly" suggests something wilful and arbitrary, and the "one track of sparkling light" makes the whole ambiguous, dream-laden scene follow after the boy and make him row so "lustily" as much out of the intensification of his "troubled" feeling as out of sheer exhilaration. He becomes a small, heroic figure beset by supernatural forces, and for several lines Wordsworth adopts the style of epic poetry in the sentence that begins: "But now, like one who rows." The boy forgets his guilty feeling and is transported into a state almost absurdly beyond himself. But the overwhelming landscape refuses to let him remain in this joyous state. It pursues him and casts down his pride. The final dozen lines, in their effect, are a psychological shadow of the action that precedes them. The night's darkness, the sky's grayness, are all that remain of the scene. Light, life, and color are obliterated. "Huge and mighty" forms haunt the boy's mind, vaguely recalling the frightening peak of the climactic lines.

It is time now to recall the stanza from *The Prelude* that I quoted first, which comes just before the longer one I have been discussing. One would have imagined that, on the whole, the boy's experience that night was very unfortunate, especially in view of the depression that lasted "for many days" afterward. But no, says Wordsworth. "A dark inscrutable workmanship" fuses such experiences into a meaningful life. It "reconciles discordant elements" and brings us through—at least if we are like Wordsworth—to a "calm existence" for which we must be as grateful as he: "Praise to the end!" He sees human experience, as poetry itself so often does, as a musical composition. Indeed, at the very beginning of the stanza, he introduces a musical image to suggest how the life process works:

> Dust as we are, the immortal spirit grows
> Like harmony in Music.

Precisely this sort of harmony marks the story of the stolen boat. It presents a music of awareness of the child's successive states of feeling as he pursues his adventure under the deepening night. Wordsworth's blank verse is enormously successful in contributing to this music. He handles his phrasing naturally, saving his pauses for points of greatest stress and thus varying the length of his breath units. The regular lines help sustain the purity of the poem's seriousness, but the rhythm is not at all mechanical. The speech is ultimately formal yet has an informal side as well, the ease and spontaneity of a highly literate person recollecting matters of the greatest personal significance. "How strange," he says, that all the contradictory experiences he has passed through should have shaped him into the man he now is. The outburst, too—"Praise to the end!"—is a spontaneous interruption of his meditative formality. More important, the long stanza describing his adventure is written in a fundamentally natural way. It has straightforward sentences, very concrete diction with strong, active verbs, and the sharpest immediacy of impression.

I cannot think of a better demonstration than these lines in *The Prelude* that the greatest poetry is closest to the common life. This is not because it says the most obvious things. Rather, it is because it brings out the actual quality of what our senses perceive and what our hearts feel about the perception. It brings out the latent music of our awareness in such a way that we recognize ourselves as never before.

Musics of Awareness:
Association and Feeling

I have been talking about one sort of music of awareness, easily recognizable because it is like the music for a film script. It goes right along with all of us as we move through time and space and respond to whatever is unfolding. The possibilities are infinite—the wild, melodramatic music of emotion that might, say, accompany the effort to land a badly damaged plane safely, or the bitterly staccato music of a quarrel, or the tedious drone of boring mechanical work. All the poems of the preceding chapter except Whitman's could be illustrated by a movie camera focused on a single dramatic setting and sequence, and each has a musical pattern directly responsive to the impacts of those circumstances on the speaker's mind. In each the music of awareness within the mind has an external source.

The passage from Whitman is different. I introduced it among the poems of time and space because, like them, it is punctuated by sharp sense impressions that give it a living body of concretely sensuous language. But its primary music does not come from the speaker's response to outside things. Rather, it comes from within him, from the inner awareness and need that have led him to seek out and fasten on details of the external world. I shall repeat only a few lines from the Whitman passage as a reminder. It is interesting that the first impression it reports, of the "atmosphere," is so negative that it is no impression at all. The atmosphere, we are told, has no smell or taste. And at once the emphasis shifts to the speaker's state of feeling, where it remains for several lines before the poem returns to the realm of keen sense impressions:

> The atmosphere is not a perfume, it has no taste of the
>   distillation, it is odorless,
> It is for my mouth forever, I am in love with it,
> I will go to the bank by the wood and become undisguised
>   and naked,
> I am mad for it to be in contact with me.
>
> The smoke of my own breath,
> Echoes, ripples, buzz'd whispers, love-root, silk-thread,
>   crotch and vine,
> My respiration and inspiration, the beating of my heart, the
>   passing of blood and air through my lungs,
> The sniff of green leaves and dry leaves, and of the shore
>   and dark-color'd sea-rocks, and of hay in the barn . . .

When he does return to concrete impressions, in the second stanza, the speaker looks first at the organs and processes of his own body. He is "mad" for "contact" with the air, he says, and so he lists aspects of his own breathing and his own sexuality that will enable him to have that contact. Often he uses figures of speech for these aspects that suggest either direct sexual penetration of nature or a way of seeing himself in terms of the natural world with which he desires intercourse: "smoke of my own breath," "love-root," "silk-thread," "vine." When he reaches the actual outer world in the final line—"the sniff of green leaves and dry leaves, and of the shore and dark-color'd sea-rocks, and of hay in the barn"—it really does seem intermingled with his own mystically lusting nature. The passage expresses a state of exaltation, a passion both sensual and inspired, that is the basis both of its larger musical tones and of the driving, accelerating, orgasmic tempo of much of the rhythm.

The movement of the whole passage is a movement of the

speaker's desiring nature among images related to each other only by his imagination. He speaks first of the atmosphere, then of "the bank by the woods," then of organs and processes of his own body, and then of varied objects in nature. This sequence of points of attention is arranged by the flow of his inward associations, all of which follow from the contrast he draws between the "odorless" atmosphere and the "perfumes" of houses. Perfumes are the result of a "distillation," by which he means that civilized traditions—and especially books —supersede direct contact with life. As for him, he "likes" perfumes but means to resist them; in the stanza before the ones just quoted, he says: "The distillation would intoxicate me also, but I shall not let it." Instead he will turn for intoxication to the open air and to his own body. From this point on two streams of images emerge and come together. The more obvious stream is the one I have been describing: the images of the speaker's body and of the natural world he wants to possess like a lover. The subtler stream of associations derives from the image of perfume. Although the speaker has refused to allow the fragrance of the distilled past to intoxicate him, he nevertheless has admitted enjoying it. Now, no matter what symbolic meaning Whitman gives to "perfume," the word has unavoidable seductive and erotic associations of its own, and they prepare us for the sexual imagery that follows. Once introduced into the poem, the word affects and colors its entire tone. It enters the excited sensuousness of the passage and hence the insistent intensity of the music. In the first stanza just quoted, it carries over to the reckless, wanton statements of intention and feeling. In the next stanza, its suggestiveness is reinforced by the crowded, pressing series of active phrases hurled at us with such entranced energy.

In their rapture at the sheer presence of the simplest natural objects, Whitman's lines recall a poem discussed earlier— Yeats's "Demon and Beast." The "sweetness" Yeats felt while he watched the white gull catching a bit of bread in the air and the "portly" duck shaking water off its back is close to

Whitman's feeling here. The chief difference lies in the utterly unlike situations of the speakers. Yeats's joy comes from the falling away of the pressures of passion, Whitman's from his complete possession by an exuberant, life-embracing passion. Another difference is equally important for seeing into these poems. Yeats reports a specific experience within a given time and space and then meditates on it, whereas Whitman gives us a program of his inward imagination—a program for a fantastically conceived experience impossible of literal fulfillment. Yet the sweet gratitude that flows through Yeats's poem, interfused with quiet resignation to old age and death, does somehow resemble Whitman's affirmative sensual delight.

Whitman is particularly adept at projecting an inner state of awareness through a sensuous cluster of images, and at finding an appropriate music as well. In "There Was a Child Went Forth," for instance, the music is at a lower pitch of excitement, and moves at a more leisurely pace, than in the passage from *Song of Myself*. The rhythm is biblical—nostalgically incantatory, with an atmosphere of legendry, and with many lines beginning with "And." The effect is enhanced by Whitman's customary old-fashioned Quaker way of naming the months according to their numerical order. As the passage progresses, this pervasive tone casts its net over all of nature.

There was a child went forth every day,
And the first object he look'd upon, that object he became,
And that object became part of him for the day or a certain
    part of the day,
Or for many years or stretching cycles of years.

The early lilacs became part of this child,
And grass and white and red morning-glories, and white and
    red clover, and the song of the phoebe-bird,
And the Third-month lambs and the sow's pink-faint litter,
    and the mare's foal and the cow's calf,
And the noisy brood of the barnyard or by the mire of the
    pond-side,

And the fish suspending themselves so curiously below there,
    and the beautiful curious liquid,
And the water-plants with their graceful flat heads, all
    became part of him.

Here the flow of feeling goes both ways—from outward
objects into the child's mind, and from the child's mind outward over everything the boy becomes aware of. Mainly,
though, it is the latter. From the start the emphasis is on the
child's inward self, which seeks empathy with everything he
comes in contact with and then absorbs it into his own identity. It is the *child* we are told of first; in the opening stanza the
rest of the world consists merely of unnamed "objects" that
took on importance as they "became part" of the child. Not
until the second stanza, after that principle has been estab-
lished, does the speaker begin to specify the "objects," at first
by name only and then with a few more evocative details
about them. The pace is leisurely, its lyricism a slow savoring
of each phrase for each object. The speaker in these opening
stanzas moves contentedly as he recalls those treasured "objects" in nature, the flowers and farm animals and fish and
water plants, that the boy took into his own nature as he
walked forth day after day. In later stanzas the list of "objects" extends to members of the boy's family and to various
aspects of their personalities and details of their home, and
then to his thoughts, and finally to a mixture of street sights,
far-off views, and sea images. The list could easily have gone
on indefinitely. The speaker's "yearning and swelling heart"
has room for ever more shared identities.

Whitman in this poem speaks very directly out of the realization that poetry is the voice of the common life, giving
shape and utterance to the chaos of impulses and impressions
that existence would be without language. At his moments of
most intense perception, it is hard to tell whether he is aroused
into musical life by the touch of reality on his exquisite responsiveness, or whether he brings that musical life to the
world that he finds so thrilling to touch. His own stress at

those moments is on a confusion of thought as he yields to the irresistible, sexual power of touch. It is in *Song of Myself*, again, that we find him writing most unrestrainedly on the interaction of inner self and outer world—

> Is this then a touch? quivering me to a new identity,
> Flames and ether making a rush for my veins,
> Treacherous tip of me reaching and crowding to help them,
> My flesh and blood playing out lightning to strike what is
>   hardly different from my self,
> On all sides prurient provokers stiffening my limbs,
> Straining the udder of my heart for its withheld drip,
> Behaving licentious toward me, taking no denial,
> Depriving me of my best as for a purpose,
> Unbuttoning my clothes, holding me by the bare waist,
> Deluding my confusion with the calm of the sunlight and
>   pasture-fields . . .

That is the beginning of section 28 of *Song of Myself*. It shows, I think, that for Whitman full awareness is a kind of agony and a kind of rapture—the two sides of ecstasy—rather than a state of quiet meditation. It is a state of confusion between oneself and the rest of life, as the fourth line states clearly. The "new identity" to which the touch of life "quivers" him is hardly the steadying, tranquil condition that most people think of when they talk about finding their true identities. It is existence under extreme pressure, with every side of oneself under assault. Section 28 ends with these lines:

> You villain touch! what are you doing? my breath is tight in
>   its throat,
> Unclench your floodgates, you are too much for me.

The next section of *Song of Myself* is only six lines long, but takes us further into the subjective state introduced by the question "Is this then a touch?" There is some ambiguity concerning the real source of the half rhapsodic, half suffering music of extreme response to the "prurient provokers" in

section 28. The music of section 29, though, clearly comes
from deep within the speaker's richly sensual imagination:

> Blind loving wrestling touch, sheath'd hooded sharp-
> tooth'd touch!
> Did it make you ache so, leaving me?
>
> Parting track'd by arriving, perpetual payment of
> perpetual loan,
> Rich showering rain, and recompense richer afterward.
>
> Sprouts take and accumulate, stand by the curb prolific
> and vital,
> Landscapes projected masculine, full-sized and golden.

The literal situation in these lines is even more ambiguous
than in the preceding section. The speaker is not talking directly about his own feelings now, but addresses the "touch"
as if it were a person. Does he mean that when he gave his
"blind loving wrestling touch" to something or someone or
the whole world outside himself it "ached" to leave him?
Does he mean the touch was so acutely intense that *he* ached
in the act of touching and so releasing his pent-up passion? Is
he talking about something or someone that touched him—
perhaps a homosexual lover since his poetry does sometimes
suggest this very strongly? But he also plays the role of a divine spirit impregnating or at least giving life to the world
rather as, in Michelangelo's painting, God touches Adam's
finger with his own and charges him with divine vital force.
The images of the poem suggest, at one and the same time,
sexual intercourse and ejaculation and a personified vision
of the fertile earth being enriched by rainfall and yielding
bountifully.

All these situations, roles, and ideas are present in the brief
passage because they are what the language suggests. Had
Whitman wished to outline a particular meaning more precisely, or to give us an unambiguous dramatic situation, he
could certainly have done so. Look, for instance, at his brief,

powerful description of the aftermath of a sea battle in section
36. It is brilliantly accurate and, at the end, horrible in the
realism of its few but telling details about shipboard surgery
in the days before modern anesthesia:

> The hiss of the surgeon's knife, the gnawing teeth of his saw,
> Wheeze, cluck, swash of falling blood, short wild screams, and
>   long, dull, tapering groan,
> These so, these irretrievable.

But poem 29 has another purpose, to hold on to the "ache"
and richness of the life process felt at the full, quickened
through the speaker's sensitivity to touch. It does not have the
desperate urgency of poem 28, in which the speaker's senses
are being seduced—or, rather, taken by force—from all sides.
The "prurient provokers" have merged with his own desire,
and now all the attention is directed toward a sense of glorious fulfillment, climactic or immediately afterward. The
address to "blind loving wrestling touch" is happy and sympathetic, as though addressed to a lover. The repetition of
"touch" in the first line, and of the words "perpetual" and
"rich" in the second couplet, links physical excitement with
values of permanence and abundance. There is a similar linking—and a remarkable technical achievement—in the number
of words containing at least two of the sounds p, r, and t in
some combination: "sharp-tooth'd," "parting," "perpetual,"
"recompense," "sprouts, "prolific," "projected." These words
help associate different phases of lovemaking with one another. Each line is divided into two phrases or breath units. In
the first couplet the opening line consists of two aroused,
highly sensual outcries and the second line of a lovingly intimate inquiry in two sections. Thereafter, the lines project
wonder at the glow of pleasure experienced and at its "prolific" results. Because the character of the experience is not
literally specified despite the highly suggestive diction, the
tone is even more mystically enchanted than if the poem
were frankly and simply erotic. A phrase like "parting track'd

by arriving" suggests a voluptuously sexual rhythmic movement, but also some joyous reciprocity between states of
yearning and states of realization that might well be a condition of spiritual revelation. (The strong sexual suggestiveness
of much traditional religious and mystical symbolism is well
known.) The poem as a whole, then, achieves a certain poise
among possible directions of feeling that implies a fusion of
physical and spiritual fulfillment. It is a song of gratification
that is at once abstract and extraordinarily sensuous, at once
a love song and a hymn of universal praise.

The vividness of Whitman's aroused awareness in the passages from *Song of Myself* is extraordinary. To project an
inward state of mind so sensuously, as though it has a body
and a nervous system of its own, is one of the great aims of
lyric poetry, but one rarely achieved with such unpretentious
immediacy. All these passages show us that the way we actually feel and think is not something to dismiss or be ashamed
of but quite literally something to sing—to make a "song of
myself"—about. Sexual consciousness is a tremendously important element in all this, not as something to be relegated to
one special chamber of our lives but as a generative energy in
both our most serious or exalted moments and our quieter
times in the everyday world of work and sunshine and ordinarily human meanings. Not that it was Whitman's main intention to "liberate" people's sexual consciousness, but he did
have to liberate his own in order to get through to the way
his own mind, and everyone else's, was conscious of life. As in
his description of shipboard surgery, his aim was to look at
actualities. Of course, finding the language and rhythm and
musical dynamics to get his awareness into poetic action was
a matter of his special genius and artistry.

The possible forms of the music of subjective awareness are,
as I noted at the start of this chapter, infinite. We can find a
simple contrast to Whitman's music in the closing lines of the
passage from Wordsworth's *The Prelude* quoted in the last
chapter. These lines are closer than Whitman's to the tradi-

tional tone of a serious meditative poem. They describe Wordsworth's depression after the episode of the boat:

> There in her mooring place I left my bark,—
> And through the meadows homeward went, in grave
> And serious mood; but after I had seen
> That spectacle, for many days, my brain
> Worked with a dim and undetermined sense
> Of unknown modes of being; o'er my thoughts
> There hung a darkness, call it solitude
> Or blank desertion. No familiar shapes
> Remained, no pleasant images of trees,
> Of sea or sky, no colours of green fields;
> But huge and mighty forms, that do not live
> Like living men, moved slowly through the mind
> By day, and were a trouble to my dreams.

Wordsworth is conveying a spiritual heaviness. His sentences are long and leaden-hearted, and the high proportion of run-on lines prevents serious interruption of his prolonged description of his soul-sickness. Only three of these lines end with punctuation that stops the movement. The first line is merely transitional, separating the narrative proper from the evocation of mood that follows it. The second, eight lines further on, is a momentary interruption before that of the next line, whose semicolon separates and points up the contrast between the reminders of the boy's normal pleasure in nature and his present state of lethargic nightmare-vision. The words linked by *d*'s all have to do with the long duration of the malady or with its vague and desolate character: "days," "dim," "undetermined," "darkness," "desertion," "dreams." The phrases themselves often weigh heavily on their lines, slowing the iambic pentameter to a weary tread. This is partly the effect of the mood itself in such phrases as 'in grave and serious mood," "a dim and undetermined sense," "no familiar shapes," "huge and mighty forms," "moved slowly through the mind," and "a trouble to my dreams." Also, though, it is because the phrases cannot easily be read quickly. In order to read them with full attention to their sound values, one must slow down before each "and" and before and after each *d* or *s* beginning or ending a word. The words "and serious mood," for instance, cannot be read quickly without our doing violence to the friction and to the braking effects between them. In the longer construction "There hung a darkness, call it solitude/Or blank desertion," this kind of interrupted movement is superbly controlled. One must speak the passage as though one were feeling one's way into its emotional state. Its music is haltingly sonorous—the song of an oppressed and haunted spirit.

Our minds are always in search of the inner depths of ourselves. We absorb the outside world into those depths as naturally as infants try to put whatever is before them into their mouths. Touching something, as Whitman felt so passionately, is a way of bringing it inside our bodies and our minds. All experience is an invasion of ourselves. Often, as in the obvious and natural instance of sexual gratification, we desire it. Sometimes our desire is in direct and reckless contradiction to the fact that the experience does violence to us, as in drug addiction or certain distortions of love. Most often it enters us below the sill of consciousness. But whatever enters is transformed by an inner process that assimilates it into our own natures just as the body assimilates food. Everything we experience is given human and personal meaning by means of this process, and we in turn project images into the outer world again that reflect both what we experienced originally and what we have made of it because of the pressure of our own memories and needs and personalities.

Poets are especially responsive to this intimate transformation. They experience a special pleasure in poetry, their own or others', that catches the flavor of something tangibly real and returns it to us changed by the impress of the speaker's own nature. That impress is conveyed by the emotional atmosphere of the expression and also by its music—its rhythmic and singing quality. Certain modern Russian poets, among them Vladimir Mayakovsky, have had this gift in a supreme degree. Another great modern Russian poet, Boris Pasternak, describes the effect on him of hearing Mayakovsky reading aloud in an outdoor café. Pasternak tells how the scene all about the little group of poets seemed to be absorbed into what Mayakovsky was reading—absorbed and then re-created as the world of the poet's mind:

> The poplars glimmered green. The limes glinted grey. The sleepy dogs driven out of all patience by the fleas leapt on all four paws at once and calling heaven to witness their moral helplessness against a brutal force flung themselves on the sand in a state of exasperated sleepiness. Engines on the Brestsk road, now changed to the Alexander, uttered hoarse whistles. And all around people cut hair, shaved, baked and fried, sold their wares, moved about—and saw nothing.
>
> It was the tragedy *Vladimir Mayakovsky* which had just come out then. I listened raptly, with all my heart, holding my breath, forgetting all about myself. I had never heard anything like this before.
>
> It contained everything. The boulevard, the dogs, the limes and the butterflies. The hairdressers, bakers, tailors and engines. Why cite them? We all remember the heat-oppressed mysterious summer text. . . .
>
> In the distance locomotives roared like the white sturgeon. In the hoarse cry of his creation lay the same absolute far distance as on earth. Here there was that profound animation, without which there is no originality, that infinity, which opens out from any one point of life in any direction, without which poetry is only a misunderstanding, something temporarily unexplained.
>
> And how simple all this was! The creation was called a tragedy. And that is what it ought to be called. The tragedy was called "Vladimir Mayakovsky." The title contained the simple discovery of genius, that a poet is not an author, but— the subject of a lyric, facing the world in the first person. The title was not the name of the composer but the surname of the composition.

"On that occasion," wrote Pasternak, "I really carried him intact with me from the boulevard into my own life." Mayakovsky, with his spontaneity, humor, wryness, and power, spoke out of the volatile, unconscious life of Moscow. The people on the boulevard all around "saw nothing," but he projected everything. They carried around their lives unknowingly—the whole teeming world that they breathed into themselves. Mayakovsky was their eyes and ears and voice. Like Whitman, he felt in himself the animating principle that imprints human meaning on each sight, sound, smell, taste, or touch that has been received. His very manner showed how this normal psychological process of conversion creates an independent consciousness within oneself, a consciousness standing in a curious relationship to the rest of one's nature that is simply part of ordinary, unconscious reality.

The speaker in a poem often embodies this independent consciousness, especially when the poem is clearly rooted in its author's private memory and imagination. And so, as Pasternak says, the speaker in *Vladimir Mayakovsky* is "the subject of a lyric, facing the world in the first person." He is at once directly expressive of, and isolated from, the chaotic mass of realities around and even within him. Declaiming his poems in that Moscow café in 1914, Mayakovsky the living man could look upon his speaker as a character he had created: a presence within himself that was his inner consciousness, bursting out of the bounds of what he had once been. In one poem, "The Cloud in Trousers," he presents that newly created self. It has absorbed the unbearably vast totality of human suffering. Now it must thrust itself back into the world with images of what life has come to mean:

> I feel
> my "I"
> is much too small for me.
> Stubbornly a body pushes out of me.
>
> Hello!
> Who's speaking?

Mamma?
Mamma!
Your son is gloriously ill!
Mamma!
His heart is on fire.
Tell his sisters, Lyuda and Olya,
he has no nook to hide in.

Each word,
each joke,
which his scorching mouth spews,
jumps like a naked prostitute
from a burning brothel.

Now all this, including the passage I have just quoted, may seem mystical and far-fetched. Perhaps it is. But I would claim just the opposite—that it has to do with something that happens, both in real life and in poetry, continuously and normally. Precisely, perhaps, because it is so normal, so obvious, it receives little attention either from people in general or from literary critics. It is a process simple in its function, elusive and complex in the details of its working. To sum up: Our senses give us a many-dimensional inward vision of the world and of ourselves. We in turn project that vision of reality outward again, after transforming it by selection, adaptation, and redirection into something humanly usable. In the process we develop a curiously separate part of our inner selves that is able to "objectify" what we are doing—to see and meditate on the difference between absolute, undifferentiated reality and our humanized version of it.

In poetry that meditating self imprints the stamp of its vision on everything it says—the tones employed, the images and rhythms selected, the whole handling of language. Again it is instructive, just for a moment, to return to Pasternak's first impressions of Mayakovsky. Mayakovsky, says Pasternak, belonged to a group of writers who cultivated "beautiful voices." Their influence was such that "the subsequent [Russian] tendency toward declamation in poetry sprang from them." The dominant note Mayakovsky struck, the whole musical quality of his performance, was harsh and uncom-promising. It was committed to a sense of reality passionately and deeply scored on the speaker's spirit. The wild excitement in Mayakovsky, his almost jeering wit, his agony too extreme to be self-indulgent, determine the music of his best work. Pasternak's interesting explanation is that "in contempt of acting a part he played at life. . . . And it was this which chained one to him and terrified one," for he was a man for whom truth held "an almost animal attraction."

Mayakovsky was an extreme example of a dramatic, mag-netic poetic personality especially susceptible to political pas-sion. His genius lent itself to the revolutionary spirit. After the Bolsheviks took power, he served as a propagandist in verse and prose for about a decade before his unconforming nature reasserted itself—both in his writing and in his suicide. To be true to himself, a poet must necessarily be guided in what he writes by his sensibility. If his theme is political, the speaking voice must still be his own, with its own range of music, and not the predictable, impersonal voice of an ideol-ogy or a party or a state—unless for some dramatic or ironic or other purpose that makes the use the poet's own after all. Con-sider the images and tones in the stanzas I have just quoted. The mystical birth image in the first stanza could hardly have originated in a political document. Nor could the anguished buffoonery of the second and third stanzas. In the second stanza, the speaker pretends to be trying to get his mother on the phone and then shouts, "Your son is gloriously ill!" In the third, a simile from the world of the burlesque theatre (which Mayakovsky loved) compares the poet's acid, awakened lan-guage to "a naked prostitute" jumping from "a burning brothel." This image of vulnerability and self-revulsion and desperate danger presents his art as a kind of symbolic suicide. Of those later poems of his that were primarily animated slo-gans and galvanized clichés, Pasternak said: "I shall never understand what benefit he derived from the demagnetizing of the magnet."

"The Cloud in Trousers" finds its own music of awareness in elementary psychic experience. All sorts of insights, both trivial and overwhelming, from the common life have entered it—for instance, the experience of being possessed by an emotion too powerful to handle, the sense of how women feel when they are giving birth, the urgency and absurd frustration of certain telephone calls, the cry for response from those we love, and the worlds of grossness, horror, compassion, and humiliation fused together in the image of the naked prostitute leaping from the burning brothel. The poem as a whole carries an explosive political implication expressed in the speaker's helpless, volatile, driven state and his seizure, by something going on inside himself, that insists on "pushing out of me." But politics is certainly not what one thinks of first, for the references all seem exceedingly private in their character. In a complex and demanding way, this poem has picked up stimuli from ordinary life and redirected them through its central emotional state: that of a man whose "heart is on fire." I want now, though, to quote another, simpler instance of the process whereby the mind picks up impressions and converts them into a driving force and music of a new kind. William Carlos Williams's brief "Love Song" uses colors, repetitions of words, and a series of exclamations to sing of the speaker's desire:

> I lie here thinking of you:—
>
> the stain of love
> is upon the world!
> Yellow, yellow, yellow
> it eats into the leaves,
> smears with saffron
> the horned branches that lean
> heavily
> against a smooth purple sky!
> There is no light
> only a honey-thick stain
> that drips from leaf to leaf
> and limb to limb
> spoiling the colors
> of the whole world—

You far off there under
the wine-red selvage of the west!

Williams's poem is not desperate but rich and full bodied. The line "Yellow, yellow, yellow" is an active image, the projection over the whole visible universe of a man's urge toward a woman he is thinking of. That universe is tangibly out there: the leafy, "horned," actively thrusting branches of the trees (whose phallic suggestiveness is paralleled by the spreading, insistent "stain of love" throughout the poem); the colors of the sky and "the whole world"; and the sunset's "wine-red selvage of the west," waiting to receive the spreading yellow. Everything in the external universe is absorbed—"eaten," "stained," "spoiled"—into the driving emotion of the speaker until its limits are reached in that wonderful image of the "wine-red selvage." This image not only receives but contains the poem's male force and suggests female response and sexual fulfillment.

I have introduced this poem immediately after the lines from Mayakovsky because, though they are worlds apart in literal subject matter, both poems so beautifully reveal the full process suggested by Whitman in "There Was a Child Went Forth." Whitman, you will remember, wrote: "And the first object he looked upon, that object he became." The child "became" what he looked upon, a lilac or a lamb or a water plant, through empathy with it—that is, by becoming absorbed in it in such a way that he felt what it must be like to be that object. And, says Whitman, at the same time "that object became part of him." It was internalized by him and re-created as an aspect of his nature and awareness. Whatever the boy in Whitman's poem looked upon he re-created through his sense of wonder, his responsiveness, his desire to be in touch with the world's beauty.

What emerges from this process is a reflection of literal reality, but with enormous differences because of the human imprint upon it. For the poet that imprint is something to be brought out into the open through language charged with imagination. To return to Williams's "Love Song," the "stain of love" of which the lover sings is like the personified "touch" in Whitman's *Song of Myself* and like the "body" stubbornly pushing out of the speaker—Mayakovsky's "I." It is an image sent back into the world out of the speaker's psyche, which has internalized all sorts of impressions and then created this new thing, this image born of the mind's interaction with everything that assails it. Where, for instance, does Williams's "stain of love" come from? To think of its sources is to see the poet's daring. His linking of "yellow" with "stains," "smears," "honey," "thick," "drips," and "spoiling" is rooted in elementary associations of the sexual with the excremental and with such richly sweet bodily sensations as the taste of honey. The idea of passion that obliterates clear vision is linked, too, with a kind of primitive or infantile guilt that makes sex and its physical manifestations something nasty and sticky. The poem reflects a subconscious feeling that the world is made up of clearly defined objects bathed in light until the sexual principle takes over, staining and smearing and eating into the beauty of natural things—*spoiling* them. And yet the whole set of the poem is not sad or disgusted but exuberant. It *is* a "love song" and it asserts desire, in an abundant sexual image that converts all the elements I have been describing into joyous reaching for fulfillment.

That assertion is present in the romantic opening line: "I lie here thinking of you." After that it is partly a question of the poem's energetic movement, the male's active "yellow" (with its clear connotation of spermatic fluid) making its way toward the female's waiting "red." The infantile suggestions of incontinence, pollution, and staining are overridden by the movement of desire and of awareness—purely melodic in the first line, deliberately gross and savage in the opening lines of the second stanza, then voluptuously dreamy, then harsher again when the word "spoiling" enters the poem, and finally—in the two closing lines—returning to the music of the beginning but with a deeper intensity. That magnificently buoyant call to "you far off there," coupled with the shift of attention to the limits of vision in the sky (and in the speaker's desire), lifts the poem to a point of ecstasy at the end.

This effect is so convincing because the successive tones and impressions correspond to actual human feelings. The varying associations of "yellow" as each image emerges are directly related to the ways in which people experience and think about love. The order of images corresponds, in a sense, with the maturing process. Somewhere along the way in their early psychological development, people are likely to feel at least some revulsion at the proximity of the body's organs of sex and elimination. It is a paradox of human consciousness that every child knows and that Yeats reminds us of in two famous lines:

> For Love has pitched his mansion
> In the place of excrement.

But ordinarily we learn, through normal maturing, to sub-ordinate such revulsion and, in fact, to reverse it so that it contributes to the transcendent exaltation of love—one of the chief points of these lines from Yeats's "Crazy Jane Talks with the Bishop." This whole development of feeling in love-experience is recapitulated in "Love Song." If you look back over the poem again you will see that it consists of three ex-clamations that carry us from the speaker's initial state of "thinking of you" through the different negative and positive connotations of "yellow" to the happy call at the end. "Think-ing of you" opens up all the implications of sex, desire, beauty, and the life force. The final exclamation resolves the conflict-ing associations into one concentrated expectation.

One last example of the poetic use of the music of aware-ness: a passage that comes at the end of Robert Lowell's long poem "My Last Afternoon with Uncle Devereux Winslow." Here we get a child's view of a dying man, each detail of memory sharply etched yet transformed by the child's emotions and character at the same time. In this passage we are given a certain amount of narrative exposition in the first fifteen lines, all in a fairly relaxed though sometimes forceful style. The next nine lines are anything but relaxed—a series of parallel constructions conveying the child's horror through their description of the dying uncle as though he were a frightful marionette—the caricature of some primitive god. Each chanted descriptive phrase contributes to the piling up of grotesque impressions. The next three lines turn our attention briefly but sharply to the child, but in a style that echoes the tone of the lines just before them. The two closing lines move ahead to a point after Uncle Devereux's death that ironically echoes most of the earlier part of the passage.

My Uncle was dying at twenty-nine.
"You are behaving like children,"
said my Grandfather,
when my Uncle and Aunt left their three baby daughters,
and sailed for Europe on a last honeymoon . . .
I cowered in terror.
I wasn't a child at all—
unseen and all-seeing, I was Agrippina
in the Golden House of Nero. . . .

Near me was the white measuring-door
my Grandfather had pencilled with my Uncle's heights.
In 1911, he had stopped growing at just six feet.
While I sat on the tiles,
and dug at the anchor on my sailor blouse,
Uncle Devereux stood behind me.
He was as brushed as Bayard, our riding horse.
His face was putty.
His blue coat and white trousers
grew sharper and straighter.
His coat was a blue jay's tail,
his trousers were solid cream from the top of the bottle.
He was animated, hierarchical,
like a ginger snap man in a clothes-press.
He was dying of the incurable Hodgkin's disease. . . .
My hands were warm, then cool, on the piles
of earth and lime,

a black pile and a white pile. . . .
Come winter,
Uncle Devereux would blend to the one color.

Here again, as in Williams's "Love Song" and indeed in most poetry, the first line not only sets the tone but states the situation to be explored in the rest of the passage. The incontrovertible, tragic fact that the young man was dying is the burden of that first line and, as it were, hangs in the air brooding over everything that comes after it. The grandfather's rebuke seems superficial because of it. The child's terror at the coming death made him feel he lived in an atmosphere of conspiracy and sudden murder. He felt like Agrippina, an absurdly bizarre comparison since Agrippina was Nero's mother, herself corrupt, living in an atmosphere of grossness and betrayal. But the comparison brings out the child's overwrought and panicky state, and it underscores the consciousness of a cruel, inevitable death oppressing an entire household.

Everything is ominous and sad. The "white measuring-door" and the fact that the young uncle had "stopped growing" are in themselves neutral details, but here they take on a strong association with death. Then, of course, the nine-line passage beginning "He was as brushed as Bayard" already sees Devereux as a nightmare figure, not alive but "animated" and almost two-dimensional. He has his blue coat, but otherwise everything is a deathly white, and his "brushed" and pressed and perfectly neat appearance suggests a dead man in a coffin. The passage really gives us variations on the theme of the presence of death in the midst of life, and is brought sharply into focus with the line "He was dying of the incurable Hodgkin's disease." Immediately after that line, the boy (through whose eyes we have been seeing everything) is shown playing with the very materials, earth and lime, of burial—and perhaps imagining how his uncle would soon be blending "to the one color" with the soil. Two moods combine in these lines, the elegiac and the morbid. The pity of the young uncle's fate and the child's overdeveloped death-consciousness blend like the gold and white and blue and black and the warm and the cool sensations presented throughout the poem. Also, there is a certain unlikely wit and humor in the passage—Lowell's comparing himself as a child with Nero's mother and his description of Devereux Winslow as "like a ginger snap man in a clothes-press" are the most obvious examples of the way he uses the comic to stress the painful realities of the situation. The prevailing tone is nevertheless one of awestruck despair, as though the poem were a hysterically combined funeral eulogy and litany. One simple way that Lowell maintains the tone is by having so many end-stopped lines. The rhythm has to obey the feeling of litany and incantation here, with almost every line a separate cry of lamentation.

There are complex elements in this passage. One of them involves the quality of the family relationships suggested—something that the whole long poem goes into at some length. Another is the precocious sensibility of the child. Another, one I have already suggested, is the tendency toward morbidity for its own sake in the passage. But the poem simplifies things by its concentrated pathos, its appalled vision, and its skillful play of tones. For the most part its appeal is direct and universal. What is more common than to have to live with and have a natural relationship with a dying person, and then to have to deal with the reality of the actual death? What is more troubling to almost any child's mind than an event of this sort? What is more natural, at a primitive level of our human existence, than to stare with fearful awe at that great, unacceptable mystery of a man's dying, and to substitute in our own eyes, as we look, an imagined effigy of him for the real person? Those amazed and grief-stricken images result from the fusion of a child's shocked and riotous imagination with the adult speaker's need to recall and repossess what actually happened. Lowell's music here, complete with its unpredictable dynamics, is perhaps the clearest example I have offered so far of the way poetic harmonies are projected from the midst of ordinary life.

Politics

Poetry, and perhaps modern poetry especially, is saturated with political consciousness. The power of the state is so great, the problems of war and peace and of human need and human freedom so pressing, that only the utterly innocent can believe themselves unaffected by political matters. But they are often, alas, cruelly affected. They are like small animals killed by cars on the highways, or like babies killed in war by bombs. As I have tried to show in discussing Mayakovsky's poem, and his reflection of the atmosphere of Russia before and after the Revolution, this whole question is hardly a simple one. Yet it is unavoidable. Each of us, however independent we feel, is still but one soul among many, subject to the world's tensions in a thousand ways. As Kenneth Fearing wrote, in his poem "Dirge," about a typically individualistic American hit by the Depression:

> Denouement to denouement, he took a personal pride in
>   the certain, certain way he lived his own, private life,
> But nevertheless, they shut off his gas; nevertheless, the
>   bank foreclosed; nevertheless, the landlord called;
>   nevertheless, the radio broke . . .

Ordinarily we do not think of "private life" as in any way political, but when some catastrophe like a depression hits a whole society we awaken to the fact that private interest depends after all on shared concerns. In Fearing's lines a harsh irony defines the issue subjectively. The poem as a whole is both tender and mocking, an elegy for a man whose very "personal" life was finally, and grimly, shaped by impersonal forces. It is remarkable how much such irony, coming from the shocked realization that one's life is not one's own but subject to processes over which we have little control—save, perhaps, through political action at times—we find in poetry. The words of Bertolt Brecht's "To Posterity," written about Germany in the time of the Nazis, express something else in addition—the widespread feeling of guilt at enjoying life's simple pleasures when there is so much terror abroad, and so many people needing help:

> Ah, what an age it is
> When to speak of trees is almost a crime,
> For it is a kind of silence against injustice!
> And he who walks calmly across the street,
> Is he not out of the reach of his friends
> In trouble?

A deep inward irritant of conscience, for all the poverty and violence and degradation of so many people, has been present in the human spirit from very early times. The stronger tendency in past centuries, naturally, was to regard such things as ordained by God. They were to be dealt with, at best, by what charity one could muster. A few saintly persons might devote themselves to the unspeakable sea of human misery, but most people ignored it as well as they could unless plunged into it themselves by the "wheel of fortune." There were always prophets and poets, however, who were disinclined to let themselves or others off easily. (Upton Sinclair's anthology *The Cry for Justice*, now long out of print, includes many instances of this early awareness from poetry, sacred texts, and ancient documents.) Shakespeare's *King Lear* contains a famous example at the point when, in Act IV,

Scene iii, the royal hero, because of his own desperate condition, suddenly realizes how it has been all along for many
of his fellow creatures:

> Poor naked wretches, whereso'er you are,
> That bide the pelting of this pitiless storm,
> How shall your houseless heads and unfed sides,
> Your looped and windowed raggedness, defend you
> From seasons such as these? O, I have ta'en
> Too little care of this! Take physic, pomp;
> Expose thyself to feel what wretches feel,
> That thou mayst shake the superflux to them
> And show the heavens more just.

Lear speaks this passage during a wild rainstorm on a heath.
He has rushed out there in a frenzy because of his daughters'
ingratitude. In this extraordinary, exposed situation, he for
once has become able to see life through the eyes of all the
earth's "poor naked wretches." The language he uses is not
angry but pitying—all Lear's anger is reserved for the ingratitude, the lack of decent respect and courtesy toward him, of
his unfeeling daughters. He has a noble and generous spirit,
and he still speaks as a man of power even though his daughters have dispossessed him; it does not occur to him that injustice is rooted in the nature of power itself. One image he
uses is particularly aristocratic because it is almost whimsical,
or at least humorous, in its description of the torn and shabby
clothes of the poor—their "looped and windowed raggedness."
All that royal power ("pomp") need do, Lear thinks, is swal-
low the medicine ("take physic") of looking at the real condition of the needy. Then it will learn to distribute its sur-
plus wealth ("superflux") more equitably and so "show the
heavens more just." That is, when rulers behave with compassion they enact the true will of God—and that is all that's
needed.

Since Shakespeare's time, and at an accelerated pace during
the past two centuries, the viewpoint of the victims and the
critics of social injustice has more and more come into the

foreground. In the late eighteenth century, for instance, William Blake wrote his remarkable poem "London." In it we are already in our own world, the world of great modern cities. Blake's lines reveal a compassion like Shakespeare's, but they unfold, too, a painfully acquired sense of the tissue of ignorance, fear, and brutality that makes compassion alone inadequate for change. Lear's outcry that he has "ta'en too little care of this" speaks well for his generous heart. But "London" is a revolutionary document more than it is a gust of sympathy:

> I wander thro' each charter'd street,
> Near where the charter'd Thames does flow,
> And mark in every face I meet
> Marks of weakness, marks of woe.
>
> In every cry of every Man,
> In every Infant's cry of fear,
> In every voice, in every ban,
> The mind-forg'd manacles I hear.
>
> How the Chimney-sweeper's cry
> Every blackening Church appalls;
> And the hapless Soldier's sigh
> Runs in blood down Palace walls.
>
> But most, thro' midnight streets I hear
> How the youthful Harlot's curse
> Blasts the new-born Infant's tear,
> And blights with plagues the Marriage hearse.

The noble pity and the ferocity of this poem are exactly matched. The pity comes through in simple, popular language, especially in the reverberating fourth line and in a few clear images: "Infant's cry of fear," "Chimney-sweeper's cry" (an allusion to the use of small boys for the cleaning of chimneys), "hapless Soldier's sigh," "youthful Harlot," and "new-born Infant's tear." These are images out of Blake's daily consciousness; they came from the sights and sounds and human emotions plainly exposed in the city. "Expose thyself to feel what wretches feel," cried Lear, and Blake has done just this.

But in addition his language hurls bolts of anger and revulsion. Mixed with the gently compassionate images I have quoted are such harsher words as "blackening," "appalls," "blood," "curse," "blasts," "blights," "plagues," and "hearse" —words that have a savage force. In themselves absolutely direct, they create a surge of physical hatred in the movement of the poem. Yet each is also part of an image of considerable subtlety. The "blackening Church" is both a literal image of soot-covered buildings and a symbol of the clergy's corruption, their acquiescence in the pathetic exploitation of tiny children. The image of the "hapless Soldier's sigh" that "runs in blood down Palace walls" is particularly brilliant; if Blake were a modern poet we would say this was a surrealistic metaphor. In extremely compressed form it projects the horror of state power maintained at the expense of slaughtered innocents. Then, in the final stanza, we see the full force of a visionary mind in action. The first two lines present a direct physical impression. The ringing line "But most thro' midnight streets I hear," enormously evocative in itself, prepares us for the introduction in the next line of a profound curse laid upon a society. That is "the youthful Harlot's curse," not only heard literally but felt as a moral punishment for what has been done to her. The poem closes with images of the results of venereal disease and exploited sex that culminate with the figure of "the Marriage hearse": the ultimate, shocking symbol of life energy infected with death at the source.

At the same time, the poem has a dimension of cold, analytical fury, a language of deliberately calm intellectuality that feeds into its passionate vision. The speaker sees that all of London, streets and river alike, is "charter'd"—assigned to impersonal profiteers to use for their own purpose. He takes note of—"marks"—"every face" and finds on it the "marks" of bondage: of "weakness" and "woe." For the sake of power and money, human joy is thwarted from the moment of a child's first cry. The speaker "hears" the "mind-forg'd manacles" that enslave a whole people. That image gives a figurative body to an abstract psychological conception—that the enslavement is achieved through controlling people's emotional responses, mainly by training them in religious superstition and conditioning them to their own suppression. That is why they can tolerate child labor, the sacrifice of young men in war, the compromising and perversion of religious institutions, the abandonment of women to prostitution, and the contamination of love's power and possibilities.

Rarely has a poet packed so much thought and feeling so explosively into so short and direct a poem. Emotion and mental power work together perfectly here. Although the two opening stanzas derive their appeal from the simple "story" of what the speaker has seen and heard on London's streets, the intellectual notes are present from the start. The apparently artless repetitions in these two stanzas expose a chilling complex of human bondage, the idea of the city as a hellish realm of enslaved and defeated souls. When the closing stanzas arrive with their more demanding language and ideas, there is no longer any distinction between intellectual and emotional phrasing. The rhyming words (especially "curse" and the grim phrase "Marriage hearse" at the very end) emphasize an abstract idea of malignant power that is also an expression of Blake's horror. All this was implicit at the start. Blake's mastery both of language and of sound reveals itself in the way the poem develops. It is more a matter of changing proportions between beginning and end than of any sudden, abrupt shift of tone. What I have called the initial feeling of noble pity also includes something darker and more sullen. There are harsh, "angry" consonants (such as the *ch* in the repeated "charter'd") among the flowing *r*'s that dominate the opening stanzas. There are abrasive consonants in the phrase "mind-forg'd manacles," the most important and telling phrase in the poem though it occurs in the first half. Later the tone evolves into one of tragically informed anger, with words that spit and hiss and crash against the vileness and grossness of the social condition. Yet the closing stanzas have many *r*'s and *l*'s, liquid sounds that parallel the way these stanzas retain gentler notes of pity from the beginning while piling up their bitterness and indignation.

The connection between any particular sound and an emotion is never, of course, automatic. A good poet sets up such associations through his key words and phrases. For instance, many of the *r*'s in the opening stanzas of "London" are found in words suggesting grief or sadness at oppression. In this particular poem, therefore, *r*'s come to evoke grief or sadness by association with the words and phrases in which they appear, whereas in another poem they might evoke quite a different mood. Like any impassioned orator, Blake mobilizes clusters of parallel phrasing and of echoing sound to give gathering impact to his speech. In the process he makes a music beyond the immediate ideas and emotions themselves, a music of the pain of existence in the world of the poor and the exploited and the psychologically abused.

The greatest political poetry is of this nature. Blake implies specific criticisms of a radically political nature, but neither rhetoric nor ideology *limits* his poem. The two basic modes of poetic awareness—that awakened by external stimuli as one moves through time and space and that derived from one's inner energies of sensibility and imagination—are superbly merged in "London." Both focus on the malignancy of social oppression as it infects the vulnerable spirits of the people. The situation is felt as something living and complex. It is a predicament for which the speaker knows no ultimate solution but which he holds in steady view and seeks to project through language and poetic form. He sees and hears things that are plain to see and hear if one is sufficiently keen and attentive and unafraid, things that a man or woman must see and hear to be fully, and humanly, alive. He knows the dismay and the outrage that have shaken people since they first discovered that being able to recognize evil is not enough to make it go away.

A later poet, Ezra Pound, describes Blake's relation to his

vision of the human hell. He sees him as a prophet obsessed by his vision but doomed not to be able to act directly upon it:

> And before hell mouth; dry plain
> > and two mountains;
> On the one mountain, a running form,
> > and another
> In the turn of the hill; in hard steel
> The road like a slow screw's thread,
> The angle almost imperceptible,
> > so that the circuit seemed hardly to rise;
> And the running form, naked, Blake,
> Shouting, whirling his arms, the swift limbs,
> Howling against the evil,
> > his eyes rolling,
> Whirling like flaming cart-wheels,
> > and his head held backward to gaze on the evil
> As he ran from it,
> > to be hid by the steel mountain,
> And when he showed again from the north side;
> > his eyes blazing toward hell mouth,
> His neck forward . . .

The scene, based on that in Dante's *Divine Comedy*, lies between Purgatory and Hell. Blake's goodness of nature necessarily takes him in a direction away from Hell. But he must follow the slow, winding mountainous ways described by Dante and referred to here by Pound in this passage from his Canto XVI. Blake, however, knows the complexity and deceptiveness of the human condition; he refuses to turn his eyes away from the evil engulfing mankind. This double perspective of his, found throughout his writings, is one of the reasons he has become a model for many modern poets. Pound's picture brings out, too, another double perspective of Blake's. As one can see in "London" and in many other poems in his *Songs of Innocence and Songs of Experience*, he is very close to ordinary humanity and completely unselfconscious about that closeness. He feels no contradiction between being one of the people and being a poet and a seer who sometimes speaks in the difficult language of his "prophetic" books. He takes it for granted that imagination and far-ranging thought are natural extensions of the common life. Pound's lines picture Blake as though he were a figure in one of his own engravings. Naked, running, "howling against the evil," he follows his own moral road that winds "like a slow screw's thread." His motion, his bodily posture, are painful and seem impossible to sustain. But his moral energy, democratic, mystical, blazingly serious, does not flag. It is concentrated in Pound's image of Blake's eyes "rolling" and "whirling like flaming cart-wheels."

Almost all the poets I have known have had strong political feelings in the sense represented by this image and by Blake's "London," though few of them are so powerfully mobilized in their moral vision. Ordinary common sense should tell us that people alive to the rest of humanity, and particularly engaged with language, could hardly be otherwise. In our century, though, we have become more aware than before of one type of "mind-forg'd manacle," the mind's deep tendency to store away acutely disturbing information without allowing itself to dwell on it. Once we make another's troubles our own, we shoulder either responsibility or guilt. But even our own troubles are hard to face unblinkingly. Millions of people have experienced violence and extreme privation and humiliation far more intimately than Blake ever did. Yet they have been too trapped, psychologically, to be able to "gaze upon the evil," let alone "howl" against it, even for a moment. Siegfried Sassoon's "Repression of War Experience," in which an English soldier home on leave detects himself trying to block out vile memories and associations, grows out of Sassoon's personal observation in World War I. The poem begins:

> Now light the candles; one, two; there's a moth;
> What silly beggars they are to blunder in
> And scorch their wings with glory, liquid flame—
> No, no, not that,—it's bad to think of war,

When thoughts you've gagged all day come back to scare you;
And it's been proved soldiers don't go mad
Unless they lose control of ugly thoughts
That drive them out to jabber among the trees.

Lighting candles at night and noticing a moth flying close
to one of the flames, the speaker thinks of men at war being
burned to death. He catches himself in the act of suppressing
his own maddening thoughts and so, later in the poem, de-
terminedly brings them into the open. This is the elusive,
crucial point at which politics, private sensibility, and poetry
come together, the point at which personal recollection and
feeling coincide with issues of public concern. War is the
supreme example of shared private experience, especially
suffering, on a mass scale.

Another British poet of World War I, Robert Graves,
writes in "Recalling War" of how the process of repression
works over the years, eroding the memory of war veterans.
Not only do they repress the particular instance when "the
unendurable moment struck—/The inward scream, the duty
to run mad." They all but forget the obvious: "the merry
ways of guns" when "down in a row the brave tin-soldiers
fall." It is too destructive for the average mind to recall the
whole "infection of the common sky" under the rule of
Death, that "patron" of "healthy dying, premature fate-
spasm." The mind must nevertheless do so, says Graves, if
we are to resist the future return of the "boastful visions" used
to justify wars. But the veteran gradually forgets, even
though he has only too often, in his own body, reason enough
to remember everything:

> Entrance and exit wounds are silvered clean,
> The track aches only when the rain reminds.
> The one-legged man forgets his leg of wood.
> The one-armed man his jointed wooden arm.
> The blinded man sees with his ears and hands
> As much or more than once with both his eyes.
> Their war was fought these twenty years ago

> And now assumes the nature-look of time,
> As when the morning traveller turns and views
> His wild night-stumbling carved into a hill.

"Happy are those who lose imagination," wrote Wilfred Owen, the most moving British poet of that same war. His poem "Insensibility" has to do with all the varieties of repression of awareness concerning the agonies of battle. There are those men who simply cannot envision what they are not experiencing, even if yesterday they were in combat and today they are on leave. There are others who are simply dull and unawakened. There are those who, precisely out of sensitivity and responsibility to others, harden themselves so as to be able to go on efficiently. And there are civilians who would rather not know for their own narrow reasons. All need to remember the real men who are being sacrificed: "They are troops who fade, not flowers." Still, Owen observes, we can hardly expect the troops to fix all their thought on the fact that they are being used as "mere gaps for filling" by the replacements to follow them. Better for many that they should lapse into "dullness" rather than stay anxiously alert, keeping a fatalistic "check on armies' decimation." Owen's closing three stanzas sort out the three basic types of personality involved, assigning real blame only to the last:

> Happy the soldier home, with not a notion
> How somewhere, every dawn, some men attack,
> And many sighs are drained.
> Happy the lad whose mind was never trained:
> His days are worth forgetting more than not.
> He sings along the march
> Which we march taciturn, because of dusk,
> The long, forlorn, relentless trend
> From larger day to huger night.
>
> We wise, who with a thought besmirch
> Blood all over our soul,
> How should we seek our task
> But through his blunt and lashless eyes?

Alive, he is not vital overmuch;
Dying, not mortal overmuch;
Nor sad, nor proud,
Nor curious at all.
He cannot tell
Old men's placidity from his.

But cursed are dullards whom no cannon stuns,
That they should be as stones;
Wretched are they, and mean
With paucity that never was simplicity
By choice they made themselves immune
To pity and whatever mourns in man
Before the last sea and the hapless stars;
Whatever mourns when many leave these shores;
Whatever shares
The eternal reciprocity of tears.

Unlike Sassoon and Graves, Owen presses his language into some knotty, tortured sentence structures and rhythmic irregularities. In addition, he uses many half-rhymes—for example, "not" and "night" and the words ending the final lines: "stars," "shores," "shares," and "tears." Such effects suggest a difficult thought process, sad and angry and off-balance. At the same time, though, the poem is essentially very lyrical, in an almost old-fashioned way. The half-rhyming words I have just quoted, for instance, are mostly of the sort conventionally considered "poetic." Owen uses some exact rhymes as well, and many parallel or echoing phrases and lines that would lend themselves to being sung—"Happy the soldier home," "Happy the lad," and "sings along the march," for instance—while much of the rest of the poem lends itself to a half-incantatory recitation, especially the closing lines of each stanza. There is also another aspect of the tone and style, the psychological frustration that bursts into release in the curse beginning the final stanza. The fury of this curse subsides into the cosmic melancholy of the final five lines. Although "Insensibility" lacks the power of Blake's "London," it has a similar mixture of elements. It balances the sense of humble reality with a far-reaching, maddeningly helpless vision of what is happening to people day after day with their own innocent, stupefied acquiescence.

Sassoon's poem focused on the struggle for self-control of a thoughtful, self-analytical soldier, doubtless an officer like Sassoon himself, briefly on home leave. Graves's poem looked back over a long stretch of twenty years' forgetting. Its special irony is rooted in the fact that wounded, crippled, and blinded men carry their war-reminders about with them continuously. Owen's poem encompasses much of the emotional range of the other two poems, but its further reach involves a particular kind of moral awareness. The atmosphere about it is quick and dense with that awareness, as if the poet were speaking not of moral choices but of fragrances and sounds and objects to whose touch he is alive. Owen here cuts close to the marrow of much ordinary human thought. More than we ever realize consciously, we choose what to be aware of and what not. If we are fairly insecure, as most of us are, or if we stand to profit from the misfortunes of others, we can find many ways to be "ignorant" of what is happening; we will even resent anyone who breaks into our "innocence" and forces reality on us. Owen's poem moves through a tangible world, moral and political, of psychic choices related to whether or not we choose to give our full attention to the actual deaths, the actual agony, the actual pity of what goes on in wars.

The problem of "insensibility," of how we become brutal and inhuman by not *looking* at what we ourselves may be doing, is an essential preoccupation of modern poetry. It has much to do with the drearier side of common life, thought, and speech. Few people have the insistent moral energy to make themselves both recall and properly identify those "unendurable moments" of which Graves speaks. In *The Book of Nightmares,* for example, Galway Kinnell presents a monologue by an American soldier remembering an incident like the Mylai massacre in Vietnam:

That you Captain? Sure,
sure I remember—I still hear you
lecturing at me on the intercom. *Keep your guns up, Burnsie!*
and then screaming, *Stop shooting, for crissake, Burnsie,*
those are friendlies! But crissake, Captain,
I'd already started, burst
after burst, little black pajamas jumping
and falling . . . and remember that pilot
who'd bailed out over the North,
how I shredded him down to catgut on his strings?
one of his slant eyes, a piece
of his smile, sail past me
every night right after the sleeping pill . . .

It was only
that I loved the *sound*
of them, I guess I just loved
the *feel* of them sparkin' off my hands . . .

Here is Grave's "inward scream, the duty to run mad," perfectly remembered. What the speaker lacks, though, is anything like moral or psychological insight into himself, or even
any clear feeling within himself of the preciousness of those
lives he has so wantonly destroyed. Kinnell starts this bit of
monologue off in a rush of natural speech full of interrupted
rhythms and crowded with confusing crosscurrents of memory that suggest the speaker's excitement and turmoil. As the
passage progresses the situation being recalled clarifies itself,
and so does the soldier's inward state of awareness. He is a
man still obsessed with the rage to kill that he once reveled in,
or at least gave himself up to, like a sexual compulsion. The
obsession is not something he himself sees for what it is; it is
revealed through his words, but he thinks those words are a
justification of his behavior. The people he was killing may
have been "friendlies," he says, but since he had already begun shooting he could hardly have been expected to stop
when informed of the truth. His phrasing is passionate and
orgasmic, not rational:

I'd already started, burst
after burst, little black pajamas jumping
and falling . . .

The pathology of this sort of behavior is familiar in psychological studies of war and in modern war fiction. The "black
pajamas" are objects of a kind of rape by gunfire, completely
impersonal as far as the killers are concerned. This is as de-
humanizing an image as the later one of a pilot "shredded
down to catgut on his strings" while bailing out of his plane.

Only in the last three lines of the first stanza do we see that
the speaker is unconsciously wrestling with his guilt. The recurrent vision he has, every night, of a "slant eye" and of a
"piece" of the pilot's smile sailing past him is associated with
a state of nervous tension that makes him need sleeping pills.
The second stanza once again returns to the tone of almost
sexual passion for the noise and touch of guns. The whole
passage, especially the closing seven lines, has a morbid lyricism. It presents the music of a whole context of awareness:
the desire to kill in itself, the excitement of power, and the
sensuous thrill—the "*sound*" and "*feel*"—of the whole action.

Compare this passage with some of Lieutenant William L.
Calley's testimony, in his court-martial, about the Mylai
massacre (*New York Times,* 25 February 1971):

Q. How long did you fire into the ditch? *A.* I have no idea,
sir.
Q. How many shots did you fire? *A.* Six to eight, sir.
Q. One burst or semi-automatic? *A.* Semi-automatic, sir.
Q. Who did you fire at? *A.* Into the ditch, sir.
Q. What at in the ditch? *A.* At the people in the ditch, sir.

* * *

Q. What were these people doing as they were being fired
upon? *A.* Nothing, sir.
Q. Were they being hit? *A.* I would imagine so, sir.

* * *

Q. Do you know if you hit any of them? *A.* No, sir, I don't.

Q. How far away were you from them when you fired? *A.* The muzzle would have been five feet, sir.

Q. You didn't see the bullets' impact? *A.* Not that I recall, sir.

Q. How do you know these people were dead when you left the ditch there? *A.* I don't know, sir, that they were, sir.

Q. Didn't you say yesterday that they were apparently all dead? *A.* I said they were apparently all dead, but I don't know exactly if they were dead, sir.

Q. Why were they apparently dead? *A.* They were lying still and weren't moving.

* * *

Q. Had your platoon received any resistance in the village? *A.* I don't know, sir.

Q. By the time you got to the defensive position, did you inquire if they received any resistance? *A.* No, sir.

Q. Had you ever been shot at before? *A.* Yes, sir, I had.

Q. Did you know when you were shot at? *A.* Yes, sir.

Q. Were you shot at that day? *A.* I don't know, sir.

Q. Did you make a check when you got your men in position, to see if you suffered any wounded? *A.* No, sir, I didn't.

* * *

Q. Did you tell him [*Chief Warrant Officer Hugh Thompson, pilot of a helicopter, who had tried to persuade Calley to evacuate the Vietnamese men, women, and children in the ditch*] that the only way you could get them out was with a hand grenade? *A.* No, sir, I did not.

Q. So then what happened? *A.* Let me retract on that statement. I hadn't thought about it until now. I believe I might have, yes, sir. I said about the only means I have to evacuate them out of there would be a hand grenade. If you have helicopters and everything else, I will be glad to take them out that way. But I had no means to evacuate people.

* * *

Q. You don't recall how many? *A.* No, sir. It wasn't significant to me at that time, sir.

Q. Do you recall the sex of these people? *A.* No, sir, I don't.

Q. Were there any children? A. Yes, sir, I believe there were, sir.

* * *

Q. How do you evacuate someone with a hand grenade? A. I don't have any idea, sir.

Q. Why did you make that statement? A. It was a figure of speech, sir.

Q. The group of Vietnamese that your platoon had, were all of them killed in the ditch? A. I don't know, sir.

Q. Let me ask you this: Did you have any saved up for the minefield? A. No, sir, I did not.

Q. Did you testify that you received an order to save some of them for the minefield? A. Yes, sir, I did.

Q. Why didn't you save some up for the minefield? A. Captain Medina rescinded that order and told me to waste them, sir.

[Note: "Saving them for the minefield" means using them to test ground where explosives were concealed. "Wasting" means killing.]

Q. And what did Captain Medina tell you? A. Basically, the hell with the bunkers, waste the people and get your people out of there.

Q. Now, at any time did you stop and consider the legality or illegality of these orders? A. No, sir.

Now of course this court testimony is not poetry, unless we consider it "found poetry"—that is, language not consciously meant to be poetic but nevertheless possessing poetic qualities. The words of both prosecutor and defendant are deliberately flat. This quality gives their exchanges a certain irony, for the material under discussion is charged with emotional implication. The rhythm of question and response, Calley's attempt to sound respectful while keeping his answers curtly noncommittal, and his repeated, automatic "sir" when addressing a superior officer all intensify and give sharply defined form to the implicit ironic poetry and barely concealed terror of what is being developed. The prosecutor, trying to establish facts and motives, brings out Calley's unstated assumption that the people he and his men had killed were not *really* people. Indeed, the prosecutor too seems slightly infected by this assumption—not in his attitudes as a man but in the role he plays as representative of the "legal" side of war and in his reserved, objective tone.

It would be possible to look at these passages of testimony ("edited" by me in the sense that I have selected them from the record and omitted more drawn-out and monotonous exchanges) as making a poem of considerable impact. At first reading one might not catch all the irony, grossness, and pathos, but any attentive reader will quickly pick up the patterns of question and response and the reverberations of the colloquial, apparently very cool manner of the participants. One might even argue that, in its edited form, this is more effective poetry than Kinnell's passage, livelier and more varied though the latter is. Like other social and ceremonial rituals, courtroom procedure can sometimes make for enormous compression in circumstances of great human and symbolic meaning. Moreover, when for almost any reason one isolates a bit of actual speech or conversation and, as it were, puts a frame around it, it begins to behave like a poem. Usually it will be an undeveloped poem, but the implicit possibilities of most human expression constitute a kind of pressure that is a most important element in the making of poems. The Calley trial was itself an expression of a volatile situation; it drastically revealed unresolved memories of the slaughter at Mylai and the political dilemma created by irreversible guilt, all through the "normal" attitude and tone of the defendant.

In another part of *The Book of Nightmares*, Kinnell luridly illuminates the kind of mentality implied by Calley's language. This passage begins with an image of a mere "piece of flesh" on the battlefield and ends with a symbolic outcry against an image of war that refuses to die away. In between we are assaulted by a chanted series of words and phrases with repellent connotations—synonyms for "piece of flesh" that tell us a dead body is but offal or refuse.

A piece of flesh gives off
smoke in the field—

carrion,
caput mortuum,
orts,
pelf,
fenks,
sordes,
gurry dumped from hospital trashcans.

Lieutenant!
This corpse will not stop burning!

One function of art is to hold on to such images of revulsion, which could otherwise sink easily into the subconscious life, and to thrust them once again into the foreground of consciousness. It is important to do so lest we forget the realities that have shaped us and that must be remembered if we are to see ourselves and the world around us at all truly. A poet seized by such images cannot help feeling that if he represses them they will work on him in secret and distort his nature, and that the same process goes on in other people as well. The political side of all this has to do with the tremendous educational tasks before us if individual perception and conscience are to be applied to the great social problems of mankind. As Blake saw in his poem "The Sick Rose," unresolved evil is an active force even when "invisible."

O Rose, thou art sick!
The invisible worm,
That flies in the night,
In the howling storm,

Has found out thy bed
Of crimson joy
And his dark secret love
Does thy life destroy.

Our need to hold on to images that horrify the memory is the other side of our need to repossess moments that once, without our realizing it, were inexpressibly dear to us. In poetry as in no other form of thought, all ideas are referred to the seismograph of inner awareness. A political idea, like any other, is referred to that gauge, which measures truth by evoking memory and sensibility. On the other hand, poetry has always been great, in the sense of "pregnant," with implied political relevance. The implication is mainly a matter of language and its tones. In Shakespeare's *Coriolanus*, for instance, a character praises the hero as a warrior whose sword is "death's stamp." Coriolanus in battle, he says, has been "a thing of blood, whose every motion/ Was timed with dying cries." No wonder William Hazlitt, who loved Shakespeare, nevertheless complained of his "language of power" that glamorizes aristocratic ruthlessness. Similarly, the ancient Greek epics and tragedies imply half-primitive values and, through the mythical histories of ruling families, certain clear political assumptions about the proper working of the state and the dependence of the community's destiny on that of privileged individuals.

We can find examples in every scene of the classics. One of the most touching scenes in the *Iliad*, for example, shows Hector taking leave of his wife before going off to his doomed combat with Achilles. The intensity of the scene is enhanced by the public importance of Hector's mission. As the great champion of Troy, he bears the main burden of responsibility in resisting the Greek invasion caused by his brother Paris's abduction of Helen, queen of Sparta. Another great scene, in the *Odyssey*, shows the reunion, after many years, of Odysseus and his wife Penelope. Its passion and rich symbolism are inseparable from the political setting. Penelope has been safeguarding her husband's domain by warding off the suitors who have tried, during his long absence, to win her and to reign over Ithaca.

The effect of such scenes is doubly powerful: the language is suited to human beings in intensely dramatic circumstances and is also loaded with the fate of whole peoples. It is a curiously related fact that it never occurred to authors before

comparatively modern times to make common folk the central figures of serious literature. That was obviously a political
fact in itself, since it meant that human feeling at its most
significant was identified as the prerogative of ruling groups.
What happens to the aristocratic heroes and heroines of the
past, however, also counts for everyone else, for they are
conceived of as embodying everything human.

An extraordinary, beautiful instance of the assumption of a
balanced, humanized universe, one based on the idea that
natural, political, and cultural order are mutually reinforcing,
comes in Homer's *Iliad*. It is the description of the shield de-
signed by Hephaestus, the god of fire and the forge, for
Achilles, the half-divine warrior lord. At the shield's center
is the visible cosmos: earth, sea, sky, sun, moon, and the starry
constellations. Around this center are five concentric circles.
The innermost circle contrasts two cities, one at peace and
one at war. In the happier city just laws prevail and there is
singing and dancing. In the unhappy city are rival armies and
allegorical figures of Discord, Tumult, and Fate that rage
everywhere. Other circles depict the agricultural arts, hunt-
ing and animal husbandry, ceremonial dancing, and the River
Ocean that, the Greeks thought, flowed around the earth's
rim. In Homer's vision there is none of the modern sense of
anyone's psychic alienation from life's accepted hierarchies
and order—only the idea that when they are violated discord
follows until things are set right again. Even war, with all its
terrors, is a means by which noble spirits and divinities struggle for an ascendancy whose value no one doubts.

The difference in our modern outlook is sharply drawn in
W. H. Auden's poem "The Shield of Achilles." Here the goddess Thetis, who has asked Hephaestus to make the shield for
her son Achilles, is shown something utterly unlike what she
expects and what Homer originally pictured. The lovely
"Thetis of the shining breasts" carries in her head a vision of
the Homeric ideal of fruitfulness, harmony, and equilibrium.
But Haphaestus has become an artist of our far-different times.

> She looked over his shoulder
>   For vines and olive trees,
> Marble well-governed cities
>   And ships upon untamed seas,
> But there on the shining metal
>   His hands had put instead
> An artificial wilderness
>   And a sky like lead.

Thetis sees a barren plain on the shield. There "an unintelligible multitude" waits blank faced for totalitarian rulers to send them marching on some propaganda-manufactured mission.

> They marched away enduring a belief
> Whose logic brought them, somewhere else, to grief.

What Thetis sees reflects modern historical experience and the disillusionment coming in the wake of the great modern wars, ideological struggles, and technological revolutions. She sees no "ritual pieties" or "white flower-garlanded heifers" or "athletes at their games" or dancers "moving their sweet limbs" in the mirror of this new age. Instead she sees "barbed wire" that "enclosed an arbitrary spot" where, without power to move or speak, "ordinary decent folk" can only watch while "three pale figures" are humiliated, tortured, and killed. The final scene fashioned by the modern Hephaestus shows the current urban world at its most hopeless:

> A ragged urchin, aimless and alone,
>   Loitered about that vacancy; a bird
> Flew up to safety from his well-aimed stone:
>   That girls are raped, that two boys knife a third,
>   Were axioms to him, who'd never heard
> Of any world where promises were kept,
> Or one could weep because another wept.

I have been discussing "politics" without much reference to deliberately political poetry of a partisan or activist nature.

Such poetry can be effective, usually in a single-minded way, because it sets strong emotions to rhythmic or rhetorical music. An association is assumed between the poem's emotion and the program being advanced. A famous poem of Auden's, for instance, is his "Spain 1937," written to show the urgency of saving the elected Republican government of Spain from overthrow by a military junta aided by the Hitler and Mussolini governments. The brunt of the poem was that this war was a focal point in human evolution. It would determine what the Axis powers would dare to try next and, therefore, would perhaps determine whether or not the progress of civilization would continue. Therefore everything had to be thrown into the struggle to save Spain. The emotions of the poem are not anger, horror, and fear, but a balancing off of pleasure in contemplating man's past achievements and future prospects against the sense of present urgency, with a certain melancholy coloration as though the defeat of Spain had already occurred:

> Yesterday the installation of dynamos and turbines;
> The construction of railways in the colonial desert;
>   Yesterday the classic lecture
> On the origin of Mankind. But today the struggle.

And:

> Tomorrow the rediscovery of romantic love;
> The photographing of ravens; all the fun under
>   Liberty's masterful shadow;
> Tomorrow the hour of the pageant-master and the
>   musician.
>
> Tomorrow, for the young, the poets exploding like
>   bombs,
> The walks by the lake, the winter of perfect communion;
>   Tomorrow the bicycle races
> Through the suburbs on summer evenings: but today the
>   struggle.

Auden later repudiated this poem as presumptuous, a reflection in part of his political disillusionment. But one can feel the thrilling, and rhetorically posed, sense of a choice before us, between the abject defeat of all man has achieved and dreamt and the new surge forward that triumph over the fascists might mean. There were other elements in the poem as a whole—comments on the heroism of the foreign volunteers fighting for the government, sentimental allusions to the "makeshift consolations" of those who give themselves to struggle, and large prophetic statements. By the time he wrote "The Shield of Achilles," Auden's view of things had become far less "heroic."

If Auden happened to read the Irish poet Thomas Kinsella's long poem *Butcher's Dozen*, written in 1972, it must have confirmed his depressing later vision. Kinsella too speaks of a world reduced to murderous barrenness. His grieving, fury-ridden fantasy, which has proved very popular in Ireland, imagines a series of speeches by ghosts of Catholics who have been shot down in Belfast. *Butcher's Dozen* begins with a scene that might well have been found on the Achilles' shield of Auden's poem. An important difference, though, is that Kinsella has deliberately modeled his style on folk poetry. His rhyming iambic tetrameter couplets are a form of high doggerel that should never be tried by any less accomplished writer. In *Butcher's Dozen* the doggerel effect created by the four-stress lines and the easy rhymes is counterbalanced by concrete language and by an intense, almost formal tone:

> I went with Anger at my heel
> Through Bogside of the bitter zeal
> —Jesus pity!—on a day
> Of cold and drizzle and decay.
> A month had passed. Yet there remained
> A murder smell that stung and stained.
> On flats and valleys—over all—
> It hung; on battered roof and wall,
> On wreck and rubbish scattered thick,
> On sullen steps and pitted brick.
> And when I came where thirteen died
> It shrivelled up my heart. I sighed

> And looked about that brutal place
> Of rage and terror and disgrace.
> Then my moistened lips grew dry.
> I had heard an answering sigh!

Poets no longer write visionary, prophetic, or oratorical pieces about a new world, a true City of God or at least of Man, which will come into being as a result of revolutionary or other political change. Instead, they are haunted by counter-visions of the kind found in Blake's "London" and some of the modern passages I have quoted. Or they hold to the old vision with a kind of resignation reflected in Ramon Guthrie's description of a Paris street demonstration in his poem "People Walking":

> They have faith without hope
> or hope without faith, or both without either.

Few poets indeed would be inspired today to see in some temporary political situation the promise the Roman poet Vergil, writing in 40 B. C., saw in the momentary reconciliation of Octavian (later the emperor Augustus) and Antony. His fourth *Eclogue*, in E. V. Rieu's prose translation, begins thus:

> We have reached the last Era in Sybilline song. Time has conceived and the great sequence of the Ages starts afresh. Justice, the Virgin, comes back to dwell with us, and the rule of Saturn is restored. The Firstborn of the New Age is already on his way from high Heaven down to Earth.
> With him, the Iron Race shall end and Golden Man inherit all the world. Smile on the Baby's birth . . .

Vergil's exultant poem, whose tone of mingled delight, enchantment, and awe is only barely suggested in the prose translation, has been subjected to much discussion and interpretation. It has even been thought by some to prophesy the birth of Christ, or at least to suggest the readiness of Vergil's generation for a new religion, to be heralded by a symbolic birth like that of Jesus. In any case, the poem does quite clearly foretell the fulfillment of ancient prophecy ("Sybilline song"). It anticipates the return of a happier civilization such as was said to have prevailed under Saturn's rule before his son Zeus overthrew him. The eclogue stands as a model of lyrical exuberance, based on ancient political and religious ideals, at the thought of a better and more beautiful world to come.

Vergil's celebration of the future has engaged his readers, and later poets, through the centuries. Shelley deliberately echoed it in the final song (sung by a chorus of captive Greek women) of his play *Hellas*, written in 1821 to celebrate the Greek struggle for independence from Turkey. Like Vergil's poem, this song begins by envisioning a new golden age just beginning. The word "Hellas" itself, the traditional poetic term for Greece, is not at first mentioned, for the play's wider concern as a work of revolutionary idealism is that all imperial tyrannies and repressive religions should die away:

> The world's great age begins anew,
>   The golden years return,
> The earth doth like a snake renew
>   Her winter weeds outworn:
> Heaven smiles, and faiths and empires gleam,
> Like wrecks of a dissolving dream.

This choral song, which has so much that is lovely in it, develops into a complex vision very close to modern attitudes. After the first sweeping prophetic outburst, the next two stanzas unfold a double view of what a renewal of the great age of Greece will mean. Greece herself—the very shores and mountains and vales and rivers and islands—will become "serener," "sunnier," and "fairer." But simultaneously the old cycle of myth will renew itself, more glorious than ever, yet reliving its old tragic themes:

> A loftier Argo cleaves the main,
>   Fraught with a later prize;

> Another Orpheus sings again,
>   And loves, and weeps, and dies.
> A new Ulysses leaves once more
> Calypso for his native shore.

Thinking of the thrilling but often unhappy associations of these mythical names, the singers shift their focus here. This stanza is a superb example of Shelley's ability to handle poetic dynamics—that is, to give us a succession of varying intensities and emotional states that carry the poem forward into its full implications. The joyous first stanza actually had some notes of sadness in it, such as the subtly nostalgic tone of "golden years" and the image of "wrecks of a dissolving dream." That image, though specifically directed against the "faiths and empires" of an undesired world of oppression, has its own connotations. One could well apply it to any state of affairs that human beings might conceive or create. Now, however, the singers have brought a mood of fear and distrust of the future out into the open, and so the vision with which the poem began grows more fragile and precarious:

> Oh, write no more the tale of Troy,
>   If earth Death's scroll must be!
> Nor mix with Laian rage the joy
>   Which dawns upon the free:
> Although a subtler sphinx renew
> Riddles of death Thebes never knew.

If the old golden age is renewed, will it not be followed, as before, by war and destruction—as happened with Troy—and by the horrors of the story of Oedipus? Troy went down in flames; Oedipus, the son of Laius, killed his father and married his own mother, each time unknowingly even though he had had the subtlety to solve the riddle of the Sphinx. Will men not trap themselves once again, just when they think they have triumphed over evil in the practical world and in their own natures, into even worse catastrophe than before? The foreboding that wells up in this stanza is muted in the next two, but becomes overwhelming in the closing stanza, which also brings the play as a whole to its close:

> Oh, cease! must hate and death return?
>   Cease! must men kill and die?
> Cease! drain not to its dregs the urn
>   Of bitter prophecy.
> The world is weary of the past,
> Oh, might it die or rest at last!

So, then, what began as happy prophecy (with an undertone of melancholy for the lost and deceptive past) has become a pessimistic outcry against the apparent inevitability that mankind will repeat that past of which it has become so "weary." The vision is thus not so very different from that of Blake and Owen and Kinsella and Kinnell and Auden. Yeats, over a century later, in his play *The Resurrection*, has a chorus of musicians confirm Shelley's fears. Yes—

> Another Troy must rise and set,
> Another lineage feed the crow,
> Another Argo's painted prow
> Drive to a flashier bauble yet.

Yeats's position was that the repetition of the great historical cycles was indeed inevitable. Each era reaches its height and then dies away in that "dissolving dream" of which Shelley wrote, while the next era begins to build itself upon the wreckage. The imagination of men is such that it first creates and then destroys each succeeding symbolic structure of desired ways of life.

> Everything that man esteems
> Endures a moment or a day.
> Love's pleasure drives his love away,
> The painter's brush consumes his dreams;
> The herald's cry, the soldier's tread
> Exhaust his glory and his might:
> Whatever flames upon the night
> Man's own resinous heart has fed.

What has all this to do with "poetry and the common life?" Very simply, these poets express the intricate balance that exists in every mind between positive and negative political attitudes. They are much taken up by the strange, confusing relationship of men's needs and desires to the way things really are. A knowledge and love of history and literature only make the irony of this relationship more poignant—when we think, for instance, of the beautiful visions of the ancient Greek mind and the situation of modern Europe. In our own day, neither poets nor other people can avoid a sense of a foulness pervading life, and a disgust at our failure to do away with the degradation of so much of human existence. Our poetry seems to be gravitating toward a wary, uncertain outlook, very often despairing of our ability to handle even our simplest unconscious drives, let alone the world's most pressing problems. Sometimes the pressures of political consciousness produce work as depressingly and wilfully destructive as the following lines by Imamu Amiri Baraka (Le-Roi Jones) in his poem "Black Art." These lines reveal a lurid variety of awareness and feeling that makes one believe a culture could truly run mad. Their racial militancy corrodes any sense of a larger community with shared ideals and problems. Various groups are portrayed as subhuman here, enemies to be denied and killed. Arbitrary, vile, and irrational as such "enemies" must feel a passage like this one to be, one cannot ignore the fact that it projects real states of mind. It shows one familiar channel—violence—into which despair is often forced.

> We want "poems that kill."
> Assassin poems. Poems that shoot
> guns. Poems that wrestle cops into alleys
> and take their weapons leaving them dead
> with tongues pulled out and sent to Ireland. Knockoff
> poems for dope selling wops or slick halfwhite
> politicians Airplane poems, rrrrrrrrrrrrrrrr
> rrrrrrrrrrrrrrr . . . tuh tuh tuh tuh tuh tuh tuh tuh tuh

. . . rrrrrrrrrrrrrrrr . . . Setting fire and death to
whities ass. Look at the Liberal
Spokesman for the jews clutch his throat
& puke himself into eternity . . . rrrrrrrr
There's a negroleader pinned to
A bar stool in Sardi's eyeballs melting
in hot flame. Another negroleader
on the steps of the white house one
kneeling between the sheriff's thighs
negotiating cooly for his people.

The despair of a Shelley or a Yeats is close to what another
poet, Tennyson, called a "divine despair." It is the emotion of
a person of broad sympathies and good will in the face of
what he knows about history and about psychology. If he is
afraid, or even if he believes, that pessimism is the only honest
attitude possible, he nevertheless does not opt for meanness or
brutality as humanly desirable. Baraka's poem, however, does
opt for meanness and brutality. The speaker in it plays the
role of uncompromising black racist. He is contemptuous not
only of all white people of whatever national origin but also
of what he calls "negroleaders"—people willing to work together with whites toward what they consider common goals.
His grossness of thought and speech, his aggressively insult-
ing tone, his images of torture and obscenity, the buffoonery
of his sound effects imitating airplane motors and gunfire, his
sarcasm, and even his occasional misspellings are all aspects of
a carefully cultivated attitude: one of dissociation from the
position of humanism that all men are brothers whatever bar-
riers prevent the concept from prevailing.

This is something different from a tough antisentimental-
ism that will keep one from being maudlin or ignoring realities. In its zeal to keep black people fighting mad and immune
to sentimental hypocrisy, the poem does violence to our common humanity. But while we can easily enough see what is
wrong with Baraka's position, it would be useless to argue
that no one holds it or feels it keenly. The poem's explosive,
volatile, murderous attitude flickers in many social and na-

tional groupings in the modern world. Baraka is closer to the speaker in the passage from *The Book of Nightmares,* and even to Lieutenant Calley, than he may think. But he provides a clearly conscious voice for one side of things in the modern world, the side that calls out from the streets with the smell of death in them in both Auden's and Kinsella's poems. The passage is a foretaste of the same world that Ted Hughes prophesies in his poem "That Moment." It is a world like that of the Nazi concentration camps, or like that which would exist after the final war, when survival would be the only issue.

> When the pistol muzzle oozing blue vapour
> Was lifted away
> Like a cigarette lifted from an ashtray
>
> And the only face left in the world
> Lay broken
> Between hands that relaxed, being too late
>
> And the trees closed forever
> And the streets closed forever
>
> And the body lay on the gravel
> Of the abandoned world
> Among abandoned utilities
> Exposed to infinity forever
>
> Crow had to start searching for something to eat.

"Crow" is the central figure whose name is the title of a sequence of poems by Hughes. He is a grotesquely symbolic figure drawn from primitive mythologies and embodying the fiercely impersonal aspects of man's nature and imagination—the aspect that will prevail if humanistic values fail. Hughes's tone of grief in the second stanza makes for a very different emphasis from Baraka's, though one no less grim. The humor in this poem, so unlike Baraka's jeering buffoonery, comes from the flat common-sense tone of the last line. This tone reduces tragic vision to a practical problem, but in a way

that makes the whole effect all the more desolate. Except for
the last line, Hughes's poem is like another one I should mention here: Edwin Muir's "Then." The nightmare images of
"Then" evoke a humanity reduced to mere suffering flesh
by the unremitting wars and other cruelties to which it is
subjected:

> There were no men and women then at all,
> But the flesh lying alone,
> And angry shadows fighting on a wall
> That now and then sent out a groan
> Buried in lime and stone,
> And sweated now and then like tortured wood
> Big drops that looked yet did not look like blood.

Thus Muir's sad poem begins. It resembles certain details of
Hell in Dante's *Inferno*, details that are equally true to the
terrors lurking in the subjective mind but not as ambiguous in
their meaning. (Muir's rhyme scheme somewhat resembles
Dante's, enough to suggest it without being an exact copy.
It helps suggest a set of circumstances whose effect continues
well beyond the first impression—a lingering painful awareness whose source cannot quite be determined.) The vision is
at once agonizing and paralyzing. It shadows forth, within a
vaguely totalitarian atmosphere, modern man's fears of being
reduced to anonymously sacrificed flesh for ambiguous or un-
discernible reasons.

The political poetry that counts may at times be polemical,
but the main point about it is that like other real poetry it is
rooted in personal awareness. Its political character is not
necessarily its main quality. Perhaps I can best close this chapter with a translation I have made of a poetic parable by Pablo
Neruda called "Fable of the Mermaid and the Drunks." Neruda was well known as a Communist, but this poem is not at
all ideological. In fact, it shares the distress of poets of quite
different political stripe at the violence that is so often done
to the gentlest and most beautiful traditions. The mermaid

who somehow wanders into a tavern, totally vulnerable despite her supernatural qualities, and is senselessly mocked and mistreated is an emblem of the politics of inner awareness, not of parties and ideologies. Neruda's harshly compassionate humor is a strange element here. It helps him avoid being sentimental while calling for openness and kindness and awe before the dreams without which no great possibilities can unfold:

> all these guys were inside there
> when she came in the door completely naked
> they were drunk they started spitting at her
> she didn't understand she'd just come up out of the river
> she was only a mermaid who'd lost her way
> their insults splattered her bright flesh
> their obscenity smeared her breasts of gold
> she didn't know about crying she didn't cry
> she didn't know about dressing she had no clothes on
> they stubbed out their cigarettes on her and marked her
>   up with burnt cork
> they laughed so hard they were rolling on the tavern floor
> she didn't say anything she didn't know about talking
> her eyes were the color of far-off love
> her arms were made of matching topazes
> her lips moved silently in a coral light
> at last she left by that same door
> she'd hardly plunged back in the river when she was clean
>   again
> shining like a white stone in the rain again
> and without looking back she swam off once more
> swam off to the void swam off to die.

Love and Death and Private Things

The desire to share private feeling with others is very powerful in most of us, though we are held back by the knowledge
that it will make us vulnerable. What we have to tell may
seem too intimate or odd or shameful or elusive, and so we
rarely define it precisely even to ourselves. The emotions expressed in popular songs tend to be rather general and to depend on their general subjects—love, death, grief, loneliness,
carefree joy—and on their melodies to suggest to the individual hearer his own train of associations. But every so often we
find a song with a special turn of phrasing in it that has its
own little secret to share. For instance, there is the great old
anonymous song, "Westron Wind":

> Westron wind, when will thou blow,
> The small rain down can rain?
> Christ, if my love were in my arms
> And I in my bed again!

The simple fact of the direct statement of desire in this
poem, of a frank and immediate sort that most people would
be reluctant to make publicly, gives it a real center. Its rhythm
and rhyme are those of traditional folksong, and every line
has a concrete image of considerable force. The apparent lack
of connection between the speaker's addressing the western

wind and his passionate outburst only sets our imaginations racing. Elementary nature is somehow associated with elementary desire. The private need of the speaker has been converted into something public and socially presentable through the medium of language.

Perhaps, linking the subject of the preceding chapter with this ever-present poetic motive of sharing private intensities, we might call the impulse toward such sharing "communal" emotion. It is a state of feeling charged with exuberant sympathies, a free-floating need to celebrate whatever is really in us and to encourage others and be encouraged by them in this enterprise.

An interesting example can be found in George Barker's "To My Mother." In part this is a British war poem of World War II, but I am thinking mainly of the way it celebrates and identifies itself with the woman about whom it is written.

> Most near, most dear, most loved and most far,
> Under the window where I often found her
> Sitting as huge as Asia, seismic with laughter,
> Gin and chicken helpless in her Irish hand,
> Irresistible as Rabelais, but most tender for
> The lame dogs and hurt birds that surround her,—
> She is a procession no one can follow after
> But be like a little dog following a brass band.
>
> She will not glance up at the bomber, or condescend
> To drop her gin and scuttle to a cellar,
> But lean on the mahogany table like a mountain
> Whom only faith can move, and so I send
> O all my faith, and all my love to tell her
> That she will move from mourning into morning.

Look at the poet's mother as he describes her here. Just *look* at her! The poet must surely have been of two minds about her. If we wanted to describe his attitude in political terms, we might say that he casts an enthusiastic vote for Mother despite some barely suppressed misgivings. Her virtues, like her defects, are democratic ones. And we might, if we wished to be hard on him, accuse the poet of unconscious condescension in this paean to his mother, who seems so clearly a woman of the people. He makes quite a point of her being grossly fat: "huge as Asia," "like a mountain." The phrase "seismic with laughter" suggests the shaking and quivering of her enormous body; and her fondness for gin, though amusing in the Rabelaisian mood of the poem, might like her fatness be a source of disgust as well. The son barely avoids calling her a great, slovenly, alcoholic, sentimental woman, given to ready laughter as one side of her too easygoing nature.

But clearly the poem has been written in a surge of affectionate acclaim that overrides all negative feelings. The chief assertion of the poem is the one at the beginning, that she is "most near, most dear, most loved." All these superlatives mark the initial burst of feeling. Barker's later lines on his mother's jolliness and tenderness and courage go with that feeling, as does the language of total enthusiasm, with a religious tinge, in the closing three lines: "whom only faith can move," "all my faith," "all my love." In the same way, the two lines at the exact center of the poem present her as superhuman, a glorious one-woman parade who is a sort of divine phenomenon in her very nature:

> She is a procession no one can follow after
> But be like a little dog following a brass band.

There are three ambiguous notes in the poem, the phrase "most far" in the first line, the use of the past tense in the second line ("Under the window where I often found her"), and the pun in the final line ("That she move from mourning into morning"). All three passages suggest that she is now dead, perhaps as a result of the bombings she so bravely, or lazily, disregarded. Barker's writing in these passages is not entirely clear, and so one *could* read them otherwise. Possibly the mother is in mourning for someone else—perhaps another son, killed in the war. Or possibly the poem can be read as a happy subconscious anticipation of her death—an unlikely in-

terpretation indeed. Consciously, though, Barker's pun about
her moving "from mourning into morning" implies that she
has been a saint in her own fashion and that now she will
mount to heavenly glory. The ending is weak, but it does add
an exalted mystical tone to the earlier one of enthusiastic but
comic appreciation. Barker's poem is a sonnet, a somewhat
odd one because of its ragged meter and its sprawling rhymes
—as though the poet's mother, and the feelings she inspires,
were too large for the form to manage very tidily. The whole
movement is a wave of love like that of someone embracing a
cause and in the process turning previous reservations into af-
firmations and seeking to take us along with him.

"To My Mother" is not a political poem, but political poetry generally has its kind of overflow of urgent empathy.
Even when such poetry is hostile rather than affirming, it tries
to employ a language and images of bitterness that will com-
pel us to share in the speaker's feelings for the time being. In
the preceding chapter we looked at part of a deliberately political poem by Imamu Amiri Baraka, attacking whites generally and liberals and Jews especially. It also attacked "negroleaders"—that is, groups that, like the National Association
for the Advancement of Colored People, do not accept the
uncompromising racial militancy of Baraka as the only way
of dealing with inequality and discrimination. Baraka's poem
is infantile and repulsive in its attitudes, but that is not the end
of the matter. It still expresses a real state of mind that, since
people do entertain it, must be recognized as present in our
lives. Another poet, Adrienne Rich, has addressed part of one
of her poems, "The Blue Ghazals," directly to Baraka. She
sees his racism as an expression of suffering and as a means of
keeping himself apart from even the most sympathetic white
mentality. In other words, her poem does not accept Baraka's
attitudes in their own right so much as it sees them with understanding. She talks of the bitterness and the maddened outcry she finds in Baraka despite his refusal of communication
with white readers, or even with white poets:

Late at night I went walking through your difficult wood,
half-sleepy, half-alert in that thicket of bitter roots

Who doesn't speak to me, who speaks to me more and more,
but from a face turned off, turned away, a light shut out.

And:

Terribly far away I saw your mouth in the wild light:
it seemed to me you were shouting instructions to us all.

Adrienne Rich's insights here are surges of identification, special ways of being *in touch*. As she says in another part of "The
Blue Ghazals":

The moment when a feeling enters the body
is political. This touch is political.

A similar moment of touch is presented in a poem of Muriel
Rukeyser's. The poem is part of her sequence called "Breaking Open," much of which has to do with her experience of
going to Washington to protest the Vietnam War and of being arrested and sentenced to a period in the Women's Prison.

In prison, the prisoners.
One black girl, 19 years.
She has killed her child
and she grieves, she grieves.
She crosses to my bed.
"What do *Free* mean?"
I look at her.
"You do not understand English."
"Yes, I understand English."
"What do *Free* mean?"

Miss Rukeyser simply gives us bare details, together with
the most compressed of conversations. The young black girl
has "killed her child" and "grieves." No further comment is
made on her character or background; the poet speaks neither
as psychologist nor as moralist. The girl raises a curious and
ironic question: "What do *Free* mean?" It may be profound,

it may be naive, but in either case it comes out of a world so different from the poet's that she can only look at the questioner, who imagines for a moment that the poet does not speak English. The girl's past behavior and present condition are just the opposite of "free." Everyone presumably knows the plain meaning of this word, yet here is someone asking— whether earnestly or ironically or compulsively the reader is not told. But the question, in all its colloquial and formally ungrammatical force, hangs in the air. Neither of the women is free, for both are in prison. The slaves were freed long ago, but this young woman has no joyous sense of being free. Her guilt is something unexplored in the poem, yet she grieves over it. In Adrienne Rich's words, *a feeling enters the body* of the speaker here, a "touch" of awareness of another person's being that goes beyond set political opinions.

Because of its particularly striking relevance to political matters, I was at first tempted to call the state of feeling I have been discussing "political" rather than "communal" emotion, although it is more pervasive than the word "political" implies. I was struck, too, by the fact that, in one of his untitled poems (part of which I translate below), the Peruvian poet César Vallejo uses the word "political" to describe just the state of generous excitement I had in mind:

> There comes over me some days an urge, abundant, political,
> to love desire itself, to kiss it on both faces,
> and there comes over me, from afar, the passion,
> flagrant, for all other passion, gentle or brutal:
> his who hates me, his who tears up the kid's notebook,
> and hers who must weep for him who had to weep— . . .
>
> whoever gives back what my heart had forgotten,
> in his Dante, in his Chaplin, in his shoulders.
>
> And I want, in short,
> when I reach that famous nerve's-end of violence,
> or my heart's bursting out of my throat—I'd want . . .

to care for sick people, driving them crazy,
to buy up whatever the merchant is selling,
to help the killer get on with his killing—terrible thing—
and I'd want to stand in good with myself
in all things.

These lines (my partial translation of Vallejo's "*Me viene, hay días, una gana ubérrima, política*") identify that essential surge of generous, irrational love that marks the "abundant, political" mood. It is a mood common to people of all political outlooks, reactionary or liberal, militarist or pacifist, white settler or native revolutionist. All experience the same range of passion shaped and shared through a common bond or loyalty or purpose. Vallejo plucks the essential volatile element, the ardor for empathy, out of its usual ideological context and shows its independent nature and force. It is love as a free energy, dangerous because it may attach itself to vile as well as to humanly desirable objects. Vallejo calls this condition the need to kiss "desire itself . . . on both faces." If we are possessed by his kind of uncontrollable empathy, we will feel it even toward people who hate and are brutal, as well as toward those whose suffering seems unbearable or whose natures are grotesque. If they have greatness about them ("Dante") or comic lowliness ("Chaplin")—and most people have a fair amount of both—we will share in them; we will participate in the very essence of their physical and psychological bearing (their "shoulders"). And the sheer force of sympathy will make us want "to help the killer get on with his killing—terrible thing." A moment's consideration of the directions into which political commitment can lead us will show that this last urge is so common that we could hardly call it a morbid aberration. It is deeply instinctive, something we need to watch in ourselves carefully and distrustfully at all times.

I am taken with this poem, which I have quoted only in part and with omissions, because it is so extraordinarily perceptive. It catches something very subtle and elusive in ourselves, a primitive impulse that colors the whole of our emotional lives. In day-to-day life we speak of the need for "communication" with one another, of what is called a "sense of belonging," of the importance of "believing" in something. When we talk in this way, we rarely specify *what* we wish to communicate or belong to or believe in. The reason is that we are thinking of a quality of experience we desire, not an intellectual abstraction (unless we mean an intellectual realization that hits us as though it were a physical sensation with an emotional charge). Poetry invites us to share in verbally realized experiences without quarreling with them. It evokes, as Vallejo puts it, a passion for "ôther passion"—that is, for the sense of how others feel. In his marvelous and tricky phrase, it evokes a readiness when one is at "that famous nerve's-end of violence"—under an emotional pressure that is "violent" because it cannot be contained within one person's skin alone. It drives us toward the impossible—an actual sharing in what is going on in the hearts of others, so that we can be in tune with the emotional energies driving all other people.

Two lines by Auden, at the beginning of his poem "Lullaby," may illustrate this "violent" and dangerous invitation that poetry holds out to us. The lines are in themselves very gentle; one would hardly wish to quarrel with their tone, and it would be ridiculous to quarrel with the literal situation they present:

> Lay your sleeping head, my love,
> Human on my faithless arm . . .

Nothing could be more tender, yet the lines affirm an elusive thought, unpalatable yet psychologically true: that such tenderness can well be felt by a "faithless" person. The speaker addresses the thought to his love, of all people. Meanwhile, though, his voice summons up the recognition and assent of all the rest of us. He assumes that we all share his slightly disturbing or shabby knowledge. Not that we are all faithless in love, but that our treacherous imperfections are inseparable from any human love.

Still, the speaker calls himself "faithless" and may mean it literally. In any case, he calls attention to a possibly unpleasant truth and yet makes it sound touching and even innocent. His acceptance of love's limitations is somehow enthusiastic—as Vallejo is enthusiastic about "both faces" of "desire" and Barker about his loving but gross mother. What Auden has seen may not be altogether satisfactory, but his language makes it irreversible and right and good. He celebrates things as they are in an unexpected way—unexpected only because it takes into account the common realities we all know about and recognize, yet have an odd way of suppressing at the same time. As with the passage in Baraka's poem, what all these poets present is a real state of mind that we, and the poets themselves conceivably, may disapprove of; yet we are forced to accept its reality and to see how, indeed, people do feel it. Like it or not, we are swept into a kind of sympathy because the genuine human note, the authentic tone of a given feeling, is discovered in the poet's language.

Take a poem as negative as the following one by Paul Goodman. It is far more drastically candid than Auden's tender lines. The speaker seems altogether disheartened and suggests that "most men" are no less "miserable" than he. Yet the kind of zest we have seen in the other poems I have been discussing is present in Goodman's "Long Lines" as well. He not only controls his own depression (a kind that most of us have experienced in absolute privacy at times) through finding a very active language for it. He also "objectifies" it—gets it outside himself and in a framework of its own, as though he were looking into a mirror and the reflection started having an appearance and life different from his. The speaker in his poem begins as a helpless, almost claustrophobic dramatic character. He uses language to push desperately against massive and stifling obstacles. Suddenly he grows hysterical. At the end he lapses into passive acceptance, wonders how he came to this predicament, makes a final outcry, and then stares quietly at the darkening stage of his own emotional performance.

The heavy glacier and the terrifying Alps
that simply I cannot, nor do I know the pass,
block me from Italy. As winter closes in,
just to survive I hole up in this hovel
with food that has no taste, no one to make love to
but fantasies and masturbating, sometimes sobbing
South! South! where white the torrent splashes down
past Lugano.
           Yes, I know
I cannot move these mountains, but how did I stray
by cunningly bad choices up among these snows?
Are most men as miserable, but only some
enough communicative to declare how much?
Balked! balked! the dreary snowflakes do not cease
drifting past my window in the semi-dark.

The speaker here creates two deliberately awkward opening sentences that act out his frustrated condition through their difficult syntax. He can hardly, it seems, muster energy to hold his first thoughts in perspective in the face of his panic. The tortured structure of these sentences, as well as the questions and exclamations and bold images throughout the poem, bespeak acute unhappiness. But the muscularity and turbulence and self-caricaturing melodrama make this vigorous unorthodox sonnet an oddly triumphant proclamation. It may be ridiculous to think of a triumphant proclamation of dreariness, but there you have it—the peculiar ability of poetry to celebrate reality. Or more precisely, what is celebrated is the *naming* of reality. When we find language that mimics and projects our feelings we celebrate a victory over oblivion. The poem is alive, buoyant, with despair.

The recurrent surprise, common to all the poems and passages mentioned in this chapter, is a frankness that shows the individual self behind the social mask. What is frankly shown is some natural quality of mind or personality, such as sensuality, that is familiar to all of us but usually either disguised or forgotten in most social intercourse. A good poem will make a space of frankness about itself. In that space, a sacred grove is created that can be destroyed only when the poet is not, as Vallejo says, straight with himself in everything. The poem is in touch with all of us, first, through the thoughts it so frankly shares with us and reminds us of. And of course it offers us those thoughts within its own dynamic confines, not as a logical argument about principles but as a series of turns on an inward preoccupation. The situation is not so much different from what goes on in anyone's head. Everyone, as it were, has the same thoughts differently. But the poet converts his thoughts into rhythmic associative effects. He may plant his poem solidly on commonly known physical sensations or desires, but he is also likely to bring in a whole set of images and tones that are his own thinking round and about the common theme. The sensual basis of the following poem by Keats, "Bright star! would I were steadfast as thou art," is perfectly clear, but Keats hardly stops with it:

> Bright star! would I were steadfast as thou art—
>   Not in lone splendour hung aloft the night
> And watching, with eternal lids apart,
>   Like Nature's patient, sleepless Eremite,
> The moving waters at their priestlike task
>   Of pure ablution round earth's human shores,
> Or gazing on the new soft fallen mask
>   Of snow upon the mountains and the moors—
> No—yet still steadfast, still unchangeable,
>   Pillow'd upon my fair love's ripening breast,
> To feel forever its soft fall and swell,
>   Awake forever in a sweet unrest,
> Still, still to hear her tender-taken breath,
> And so live ever—or else swoon to death.

No contrast could be sharper than that between the coldly beautiful relationship of evening star and earth envisioned at the beginning and the sensual lover's dream of being "pillow'd" forever on his "fair love's ripening breast." The speaker imagines that the star has human qualities. It is "steadfast," for it not only appears to hold steady in the sky but also, in its personification as earth's worshiper, is "watching" over it with sleepless devotion. The earth too is personified; its tides have a "priestlike task," its shores are "human," and the snow on it is a "mask" over the face of the landscape. So the "gazing" star is a sort of holy lover, ever faithful over the cosmic reaches of space. But no human being could be as silent and unmoving as a fixed star. The contrast suggests that the speaker cannot be as "steadfast" in the human sense either. The idea of the star as "Nature's patient, sleepless Eremite" (a hermit or holy man isolated from other people and holding constant vigil over what he adores) presents a conception of unwavering loyalty beyond our capacities. Auden's phrase, "human on my faithless arm," might almost have been intended both to mock Keats's image and to bring out a thought Keats implies without dwelling on it. Indeed, the whole opening stanza in Auden's "Lullaby" stresses the temporary, mortal character of love and beauty as if to give another turn to Keats's poem:

> Lay your sleeping head, my love,
> Human on my faithless arm;
> Time and fevers burn away
> Individual beauty from
> Thoughtful children, and the grave
> Proves the child ephemeral:
> But in my arms till break of day
> Let the living creature lie,
> Mortal, guilty, but to me
> The entirely beautiful.

And, in fact, Keats does reject any thought of being steadfast and pure as the bright star. After he has developed the chaste vision of stellar devotion to an earth purified by priestly tidal ablutions—an imagery that culminates in the absolutely chill and impersonal phrase "snow upon the mountains and the moors"—the speaker says, firmly: "No." He does want to be "still steadfast, still unchangeable," but all the terms are different now: no far-off starlit landscape but a woman's bosom, with "its soft fall and swell"; no hermit calm but a "sweet unrest"; no eternal silence but the sound of the woman's "tender-taken breath"; and a warm intensity that has in it the essence of mortality—"or else swoon to death."

In the light of this ending we must look again at the first eight lines of the sonnet. At first they seemed both elegant and slightly sentimental. Their personification of star and earth would be a brilliant yet finally mawkish effort if the octave were the whole poem. Now, though, it is clear that the poem introduces the ideal of the star's "lone splendour" and unblinking vigil over the earth partly in order to move from a false image of adoration to a true one. The true image is that of lover and beloved in a rapturous, profanely human, and precarious posture. Without the tone of worshipful distance introduced at the start, the poem would too abruptly enter its fleshly daydream despite some exquisite phrasing. But the opening has allowed the speaker to suggest, in an exalted way, the rapt contemplation of a human form before more directly erotic language takes over at the end. An "unbecoming" physical obsession has thus been associated with images that appear to suggest an opposite feeling but which have, all the time, masked the same obsession. In fact, the word "mask" is actually used in line seven. It clearly suggests that the pure white snow covering the earth hides a different sort of reality than the "gazing" star can see.

The impulse to reveal and share things that everyone knows but no one ordinarily talks about—to name them and celebrate them and cast them loose in the context of a developed poem —is one of the most human motives of lyric poetry. Before there was any large body of such poetry, in anything like the modern sense, poets were discovering and being guided by that confessional impulse. One of the truly vivid poems of the sixteenth century, Sir Thomas Wyatt's "They flee from me that sometime did me seek," is a perfect example of the process:

> They flee from me that sometime did me seek
> With naked foot, stalking in my chamber:
> I have seen them gentle, tame, and meek,

That now are wild, and do not remember
That sometime they put themselves in danger
To take bread at my hand; and now they range
Busily seeking with a continual change.

Thanked be fortune it hath been otherwise
Twenty times better; but once, in special,
In thin array, after a pleasant guise,
When her loose gown from her shoulders did fall,
And she me caught in her arms long and small,
Therewithal sweetly did me kiss,
And softly said, "Dear heart, how like you this?"

It was no dream; I lay broad waking:
But all is turnéd, thorough my gentleness,
Into a strange fashion of forsaking;
And I have leave to go of her goodness,
And she also to use new-fangleness.
But since that I so kindély am servéd,
I would fain know what she hath deservéd.

The modern reader will be struck by the spontaneous directness of this poem, though so many of its phrases and attitudes come from a world far different from ours, the world of aristocratic gallantry that existed in Britain over four centuries ago. The first and last stanzas are brilliant examples of the fashionable poetry of Wyatt's day: witty, ironic, paradoxical—a play of clever badinage on the standard subject of so much Renaissance poetry, the fickleness of women. They are brilliant because of their naturalness and because of a very convincing intensity of feeling they reveal. The imagery of the first stanza and the straightforward, completely colloquial speech of the third are especially effective. But the middle stanza outdoes the other two in both respects while giving us a stirring yet highly civilized closeup of a moment of sensual passion. There is nothing sentimental in the second stanza. On the contrary, the speaker is possibly just a little self-mocking. And his picture of the woman who "therewithal sweetly did me kiss" suggests that her charming question—"Dear heart, how like you this?"—comes from a person with a lively, endearingly humorous mind. Nevertheless, the middle stanza breaks out of the conventional tone of sixteenth-century courtly poetry, in which lovers complain cleverly about their mistresses' cruelty. Instead, it startles us with a real memory, a scene in which two living, breathing people made love. The memory means a great deal to the speaker. He thanks not God, but "fortune," for that lovely moment of sudden passion. In conventional thought it would be un-Christian of him to praise God for sexual joy. Still, he is devoutly thankful for an ecstasy that rivals, in its worldly way, that which Keats envisions.

Seen in the light of this middle stanza, the opening stanza grows more intense. Because of the ambiguous "they" with which the poem begins, the bearing of this opening stanza is not quite clear on the first reading. Literally, "they" are animals of some sort, who used to come tamely to the speaker to eat from his hand. They have changed, he says. They have grown "wild" and forgetful. But what sort of animals were these really? Certain words and phrases give the game away almost immediately. "Naked," for example, has a sensual force that shows the speaker is thinking of lovers, not pet animals. "Stalking" suggests predatory animals, perhaps, but the phrase "stalking in my chamber" evokes a different kind of hunt. So does the language at the very end of the stanza: "and now they range/ busily seeking with a continual change." Put all these expressions together and you have a picture of restlessly promiscuous people, faithless lovers and mistresses. If the "they" still leaves us in doubt whether the speaker is thinking of animals after all, or lovers in general, or perhaps even friends or political supporters who have proved untrustworthy, the second stanza makes all clear. "They" turns into "she," and we can now see that the first stanza was about his mistress, in particular, as the embodiment of female changeableness. The words and phrases I have mentioned prepare us for this meaning from the start. They are too heady and personal to be ignored, despite the speaker's general tone of sophisticated cynicism, and they point toward the love scene he remembers.

The very first line of the closing stanza—"It was no dream; I lay broad waking"—again focuses our attention on the marvel and the literal truth of the memory of that same scene. Then the speaker breaks out of his trance, as it were. In a series of sardonic gibes, he says just what he feels about his lost mistress. But the pain, bitterness, and humiliation keep the ending from being gracefully clever. The experience remembered in the second stanza was too gratifying and happy for easy dismissal, and at the end the lover is complaining in an awkwardly personal way as though he were talking the whole thing over with a close friend. His language is perfectly natural for his time, so natural and casual that it eludes my attempt to rephrase the last stanza in modern English prose and still keep the same flavor. A rough version would go something like this: *It wasn't a dream; I was wide awake. But everything has been turned—because of and perhaps in spite of my being a gentleman—into a reason for following a strange new fashion of walking out on each other. I have her generous permission to go my own way, and she feels free to try these newfangled ways. But since she has served me so kindly and characteristically, I'd like to know what I owe her in return.* I am sure I could improve on this unsatisfactory "translation" of mine, but not enough to catch the intimate voice of the living poem. I have tried to suggest that in Wyatt's time words like "gentleness" and "kindly" were in transition from earlier meanings to their modern ones, but that is not the whole problem. The second and third lines of the stanza are so idiomatic that, although we can feel their wry wit and ruefulness, they are as hard to paraphrase as though they were written in highly colloquial French. The play on "servéd" and "deservéd" would seem forced in modern English, an equivalent of using "served" and "disserved" in place of those two words. Even the word "dream" in the first line alludes partly to a form of literature that is now virtually obsolete.

The basic meaning and mood come across to us today, never-theless. The betrayed lover's sensual memories and his present dismay assert themselves and carry us with him despite the original obstacles of a rather stylized literary tradition and despite the later obstacles created by changes in the language.

At a distance of more than four centuries we can see that Wyatt's poem reveals and seeks to magnetize us into follow-ing the grain of his inner nature within the cultural grain of his times. This is the essential rhetorical purpose of lyric po-etry, a discovery for the reader or listener of the organic rhythm and sense, the very touch, of private experience—a reaffirmation of the reality that everyone feels within himself but is never sure that others do also: as Whitman says, "the common air that bathes the globe." Poem 11 of Whitman's *Song of Myself*, which is based on extraordinary sexual em-pathy, may serve as an instance of this reaffirmation:

> Twenty-eight young men bathe by the shore,
> Twenty-eight young men and all so friendly;
> Twenty-eight years of womanly life and all so lonesome.
>
> She owns the fine house by the rise of the bank,
> She hides handsome and richly drest aft the blinds of the
>   window.
>
> Which of the young men does she like the best?
> Ah the homeliest of them is beautiful to her.
>
> Where are you off to, lady? for I see you,
> You splash in the water there, yet stay stock still in your
>   room.
>
> Dancing and laughing along the beach came the twenty-
>   ninth bather,
> The rest did not see her, but she saw them and loved
>   them.
>
> The beards of the young men glisten'd with wet, it ran
>   from their long hair,
> Little streams pass'd all over their bodies.
>
> An unseen hand also pass'd over their bodies,
> It descended tremblingly from their temples and ribs.

> The young men float on their backs, their white bellies
>   bulge to the sun, they do not ask who seizes fast to
>   them,
> They do not know who puffs and declines with pendant
>   and bending arch,
> They do not think whom they souse with spray.

The poem begins with a boldly simple scene. It has potentialities for pathos and for ribald comedy at the same time,
but the gentleness of the language and the word "lonesome"
modulate it toward pathos and something more—human sympathy that takes the scene beyond caricature. Almost at once
the poem shows its double viewpoint. It speaks actively for
the young men and even more so for the woman watching
them from her window. They bathe unconsciously, while she
looks on with curiosity and desire. We see them first, then
quickly shift to her and follow her eyes and her imaginings.
These take us back to an extremely sensuous closeup that
frames the swimmers as in a painting and at one and the same
time presents their pleasure in what they are doing and her
view of them in the sunlight:

> The beards of the young men glisten'd with wet, it ran
>   from their long hair,
> Little streams pass'd all over their bodies.

The final two stanzas move back and forth between the
two centers of attention, with an ever-increasing sexual emphasis. Her "unseen hand" caresses them as she joins them in
her longing imagination. They "float on their backs" and she
feels she is among them making love with all of them, though
"they do not know who puffs and declines with pendant and
bending arch." The speaker in the poem feels the woman's
secret need and presence so keenly that he compels us to
abandon any stereotyped response we may have felt to the
initial scene. Doubtless Whitman's homosexuality makes itself felt in the whole developing excitement of this poem, but
on the surface that is not the point at all. The focus is on the
natural physicality of the young men and on the woman's

erotic fascination by them. In an earlier chapter I had occasion to note Whitman's extreme sensitivity and vulnerability to touch, manifested in other parts of *Song of Myself*. Here we have a supreme instance of shared or communal emotion reached through insight into people's "concealed imaginings" (a phrase of Wallace Stevens's). A political use might conceivably be made of this poem, if one were advocating free attitudes toward sexuality, as in a remote sense Whitman is indeed doing here. Each of the little stanzas is a stab of identification that carries us more surely into an ambiguous state of awareness completely outside ordinary moral considerations, especially if we remember that this is a poem of the last century.

The impulse of which I have been speaking, the need to follow through on a quite private insight until it completes itself in a poem that is both a world unto itself and a window into everyone's secret mind, is doubtless the chief link between poetry and the common life. I half believe that it underlies all communication and all rhetoric, and that it is far more important than any overt system of principles and beliefs. The starting point, the kernel, is always something plain and yet "unsayable." Williams has a poem called "Death" that begins outrageously:

> He's dead
> the dog won't have to
> sleep on his potatoes
> any more to keep them
> from freezing
>
> he's dead
> the old bastard—
> He's a bastard because
>
> there's nothing
> legitimate in him any
> more
>   he's dead
> He's sick-dead

                              he's
                a godforsaken curio
                without
                any breath in it

                He's nothing at all
                        he's dead
                shrunken up to skin

                              Put his head on
                one chair and his
                feet on another and
                he'll lie there
                like an acrobat—

                Love's beaten. He
                beat it. That's why
                he's insufferable . . .

One just doesn't say these things, yet it soon becomes clear that Williams's poem is a reaction of love. It expresses the sense of betrayal we feel when a loved person dies. Even if we were not close to him, the feeling of dismay and anger would be there because of our helplessness to do anything about it. The precious facts of anyone's life, even the ludicrous details of the kind that make up most of the first stanza, are no longer applicable, whether to be cherished or as a source of irritation. The corpse is an object, not a person—hence the helpless clowning of the sixth stanza, just before the basic feeling of the poem is expressed in the quick complaint: "Love's beaten." The point is that one cannot get around the fact given in the flat opening statement: "He's dead." This statement becomes the poem's refrain, repeated at strategic points along the way. As the poem progresses it becomes both a reiterated lament and an ironic comment on our insistence that the dead man remain a person in our minds, a "he" about whom meaningful thoughts can be entertained. But the essential obstacle of the irreversible fact remains, and its painful reality carries over into all the other statements using the contraction "he's" or any form of the pronoun "he." The rhythm of the whole poem arranges itself ritually around the recurrence of "he" and "he's," which come to have all grief in them by the end of the poem despite the deliberately brutal surface tone. And of course the poem is insisting that we not hide the essential fact or try to talk it out of existence, that we not yield to any supposedly consolatory effort to gloss over the loss.

Under ordinary circumstances such an insistence on isolating and stressing the fact that hits the senses hardest would be thought morbid, an accusation quite often leveled at poets when they focus on death or suffering. Seeming morbid, or prurient, or hyper-responsive is a risk that goes with heightened awareness and with the mobilization of language and rhythm to express it. But it is really only the result of the time-honored need and duty of poets to use language cleanly and clearly and with all its right associations intact—to use it for all it is worth and to be the sounding boards of sensibility in their time. At any rate, they can hardly be compelled to suppress their own perceptions except at the expense of their own art and of the clarification of otherwise unrealized common feelings. On the simplest practical level, it is after all useful to know how people, and not just poets, feel inwardly in circumstances of emotional arousal or stress. Ramon Guthrie, for instance, tells us in "Today Is Friday" how it feels to be mortally ill with cancer:

> You could taste it being fed intravenously through a
> skein of tubes into your most plausible dreams
> It was happening   It was going on as suavely
> as if it were a rank of drop-forges
> smashing diamonds to dust as fast as
> they could be fed to them.
>
> Tangible
> It is a great protracted
> totally transparent cube
> with sides and angles
> perceptibly contracting against
> eyeballs and nose and mouth and skin

It is always happening
It is always going on
When it gets tired of going on
maybe it will stop

It is characteristic of such writing, however, that in addition to its literal report on subjective feelings it is also, always, unpredictable and that it gathers many perspectives around it and organizes them within its own "system." Even in this passage from Guthrie's poem we can see the poet discovering the pattern within his own suffering that he can share with others. The passage reports the terrible ceaselessness of his disease—its total invasion of his mind and body in the first quoted stanza, its palpable presence in the hallucination that he is being pressed and stifled by a constantly contracting "totally transparent cube" in the second, and its tirelessness in the third. Images from hospital experience and industrial process come together, each presenting a new impression of the endless process of the body's self-destruction. The speed and intensity and unavoidability of the process are hideous; yet the notion of controlled patterns gone wild, reflected in the images of "drop-forges/ smashing diamonds to dust" and of the murderous invisible cube, has a certain order and beauty. The speaker relates himself to more than his illness while conceding its power. The death process, the eternal process of destructive change, the unending assault on the body and breaking down of individual consciousness into impersonal cosmic patterns (as in the oppressive image of the contracting cube) are inseparable from being alive; when they come to an end so does life. There is a kind of personally tragic triumph in Guthrie's creation of a poetic form that embodies the fierce unending pressure of existence on the individual life. The absence of punctuation except where absolutely necessary for clarity is a device for suggesting that the destructive pressure never stops. Its swiftness and pervasiveness and irreversibility make for a multiple imagery of terror caught in action.

To be able to find the rhythmic pace and pitch of diction that will be keyed to the curve of movement involved in exploring such essential realizations is one mark of high artistry. This is especially true when the poet piles diverse images, at first apparently unrelated, on one another in a cumulatively coherent pattern. The images are projected to give the poem its bearings as it moves into its exploration, for what it has to say is not just a generalization—that, for instance, it is frustrating to feel isolated (Goodman), or that faithless people can be tender lovers (Auden), or that lovers long to have their joy endure forever (Keats). What is said is always something quite particular, not an idea but a condition of feeling that exists in the shape and suggestion of the language as it flows and erupts and shifts direction in the poem. We cannot disagree with a poem. We can only recognize or miss states of realization within it that show us the hidden life we all live. The sense of a mind or sensibility or body in motion is often deeply present in those states, as the passage from Guthrie's poem, among many other passages I have quoted, shows. But we might just pause over a few examples suggesting the power of the sense of motion, or of an enforced pause for a moment in the midst of motion, in bringing a poem to its discovery. Thus, a passage in Hart Crane's mystical sequence *Voyages*, in which the sea is perceived as a vast emblem of sexuality— again, as in Whitman's "Twenty-eight young men," with ambivalent overtones—presents a moment of ecstasy in love in the midst of every kind of continuous motion. It is a moment held so intensely within that motion that it seems to the speaker to transcend time and death:

> And so, admitted through black swollen gates
> That must arrest all distance otherwise,—
> Past whirling pillars and lithe pediments,
> Light wrestling there incessantly with light,
> Star kissing star through wave on wave unto
> Your body rocking!
>   and where death, if shed,

> Presumes no carnage but this single change,—
> Upon the steep floor flung from dawn to dawn
> The silken skilled transmemberment of song . . .

Keyed to intense feeling, the language leaps ahead of the reader in all the connections it finds between images of sea and light, suggestions of the sexual act, depths and heights of emotion, and the fusion of all these motifs in "the silken skilled transmemberment of song." The speed of association, and of the various kinds of movement—"whirling," "wrestling," "kissing," "rocking," "shed," "flung"—indicated by the verbs, brings us into the world of the poem's awareness and compels us to become part of it. We cannot begin to respond to the poem unless we allow this to happen. When it does, we are ready for the rather complex subjective state that Hart Crane reveals in *Voyages*. That state includes fear of adult love and of life's elemental realities and, at the same time, the overcoming of fear by a daring plunge into the forbidden and the unknown. The reader who allows himself to be transported by the rush of language into the world of *Voyages* enters a state of vulnerability and risk recognizable to almost everyone in at least some of its myriad guises.

Such a state is often undefinable except through images and tonal associations, and yet the speaker's urgent need to share it with us is evident. Though externally inexpressible, it is inwardly a very sharply defined situation, so pressing that it cannot be kept purely private. Energetic movement, quite apart from everything else in the poem, may be the primary clue to us of this fierce pressure. The beginning of Emily Dickinson's " 'Twas like a Maelstrom, with a notch" is a classic instance. The speaker here is a person who has been almost paralyzed by an impossible moral and psychological predicament, something she cannot bring herself to describe except in terms of how it felt. Throughout the poem, though the imagery hints at an unbearable conflict between passion and puritanical guilt, the predicament is never named except as the implied subject in the opening word, " 'Twas":

> 'Twas like a Maelstrom, with a notch,
> That nearer, every Day,
> Kept narrowing its boiling Wheel
> Until the Agony
>
> Toyed coolly with the final inch
> Of your delirious Hem—
> And you dropt, lost,
> When something broke—
> And let you from a Dream . . .

Whatever "it" was, there was nothing static about it. It was "like a Maelstrom," and we must imagine its victim (the "you" of the poem—an interesting pronoun, since the speaker seems to mean "I") swirling helplessly at its center until such time as the "boiling wheel" narrows enough to pull her under and drown her. As with the Hart Crane passage, very active verbs draw us into the frantic scene in which the word "Agony" applies both to the maelstrom and to the victim's experience. Just as she is about to be "dropt, lost," into the whirlpool's depths, the nightmare situation ends. The images of "a Maelstrom with a notch" and a "delirious Hem" may suggest a woman's guiltily aroused sexual desire, from whose consequences circumstance or inhibition save her at the last minute. This possibility is sustained by the succeeding images in the poem paralleling that of maelstrom and victim. These are, first, a fiendish "goblin's" huge hand, about to crush her, and, second, a hangman's noose. In these instances, too, she is reprieved. But the question she asks at the end shows that the fate she had been about to suffer would have been a surrender to something desirable even if it should fill her with remorse and guilt:

> Which Anguish was the utterest—then—
> To perish, or to live?

The predicament, for a virtuous but passionate lady of the nineteenth century (perhaps not a very different sort of person from the lady in Whitman's poem), might well seem tormenting and obvious. At any rate, the speed of the closing-in movement in the opening lines, and then the sudden halt in the moment of release, have a great deal to do with the sense of imminent disaster and psychic confusion in the passage, whether or not the literal situation is spelled out for us. As the poem stands, we may speculate as we will about the kinds of personal crisis and of torturing, fearful anticipation its language may evoke. Each of us will have his or her set of memories of moments awaited half in dread, half in hope—challenges that filled us with panic though, after all, we would regret not having had to meet them.

My final example of the use of imagery of motion in setting up a poem's emotional dynamics is Sylvia Plath's "Ariel." This poem brings together three kinds of experience—riding a horse, sexual climax, and the impulse toward death or suicide. That is, it presents a complex emotional state in which the succession of sensations and images comes from these sources. Starting with "stasis in darkness," a condition of stillness and unresolved possibility before the poem's pure curve of movement toward the sunrise that brings it to an end ("the red/Eye, the cauldron of morning"), the action reaches one climactic height after another until the drastic final image. The vague pre-dawn light that appears in the sky after the very early morning's darkness is "substanceless." The speaker and whatever she is engaged with are all, so it seems, that is substantial in the universe. The ecstatic horseback ride that sounds at the same time like lovemaking (or the ecstatic lovemaking that sounds at the same time like horseback riding) brings her to a state of climax in which she sheds her old self and feels herself orgasmically "foam to wheat, a glitter of seas"—the images suggest richness and beauty, but also transformation into something impersonal. She experiences the sense of having conceived ("The child's cry/ Melts in the wall"—presumably the absorption into the womb of the child destined to be born). But at this most climactic moment a new element enters the poem. The female speaker becomes a male force, "arrow" or sperm ("dew that flies") into the great ovum-like "red eye" of the morning sun. If one could actually penetrate the sun, it would mean death, and so she has become "suicidal," self-destructive, as a result of her sense of total exaltation and self-transformation:

> Stasis in darkness.
> Then the substanceless blue
> Pour of tor and distances.
>
> God's lioness,
> How one we grow,
> Pivot of heels and knees!—The furrow
>
> Splits and passes, sister to
> The brown arc
> Of the neck I cannot catch,
>
> Nigger-eye
> Berries cast dark
> Hooks—
>
> Black sweet blood mouthfuls,
> Shadows.
> Something else
>
> Hauls me through air—
> Thighs, hair;
> Flakes from my heels.
>
> White
> Godiva, I unpeel—
> Dead hands, dead stringencies.
>
> And now I
> Foam to wheat, a glitter of seas.
> The child's cry
>
> Melts in the wall.
> And I
> Am the arrow,
>
> The dew that flies
> Suicidal, at one with the drive
> Into the red
>
> Eye, the cauldron of morning.

Underlying everything else in "Ariel" is its feeling of a glowing, speeding arc of sheer intensity that is so keen it cannot be contained within life's normal limits. The "stasis in darkness" suggests a depressive condition out of which the escalation of feeling rises with manic excitement toward self-destructive illusions of power. From being momentarily thwarted the feeling gathers a greater and greater assurance until the speaker imagines that she has stripped her spiritual self naked and can become whatever she wills. When she becomes "at one" with the great force of the universe outside herself she will have obliterated her former nature entirely. The stanzas are a very free adaptation of Dante's *terza rima*, which has the double advantage of making each stanza a relatively brief independent unit of movement and emotional focus while providing continuity, through rhyme echoes and sentences that flow from one stanza to the next, of impulse throughout the poem. The very common psychological condition of manic elation that can easily turn into its opposite is beautifully clarified in this remarkable poem. Once we are touched by its racing dynamics, its successive moments of awareness command our empathy as long as the movement lasts. These are effects heightened by the enormously intensified responsiveness of the speaker in her sensitized state.

The examples of the present chapter have brought my book full circle—for the time being at least, for the proliferations of the subject have grown on me while I was pursuing it. The temptation is to take every interesting poem that I know as a new example, secure in the knowledge that it will add something to my thoughts in a surprising way. Common speech, common awareness, are both the soil and the substance of the most absorbing poetry. When, as in "Ariel" and most other poetry of some power, both imagination and diction go beyond the way people ordinarily talk, they are nevertheless very much in touch with the rhythms of spoken language and the floating images of general consciousness. The memory of moments charged with utmost significance

for the speaker animates these poems and makes them brilliant. The power of such poems is directly related to their
overwhelming need to create empathy in the reader and so
recruit him to recognition of their inmost emotional discovery. Speaking in his poem "Burnt Norton" of the persistent
memory one has of experiences desired but never achieved,
T. S. Eliot tells his reader very simply how that empathy
comes about:

> Footfalls echo in the memory
> Down the passage which we did not take
> Towards the door we never opened
> Into the rose-garden. My words echo
> Thus, in your mind.

There is another discovery. I close this book with reluctance, knowing how much more there is to find out simply
for the asking, just by looking once again at the next real
poem that comes echoing down my memory . . .

A Note on the Quotations

All the twentieth-century poetry and prose I have quoted can be found in the books listed below. The list is alphabetical, by author. It names the best available editions in which American and British readers can find the work I have discussed.

For work written before our century, a list is not really needed. From Wyatt and Shakespeare to Whitman, the poetry I have quoted is easy to come by in many editions and anthologies; and the chief scholarly editions are cited in many studies and reference works. My two exceptions are Vergil and Emily Dickinson. I list Vergil because I have used a particular modern translation, and Emily Dickinson because she has such a tangled publishing history that the only inclusive and relatively reliable edition is the one noted here.

Interested readers should be on the lookout for paperback selected editions, which flicker on and off like fireflies in the ghost-world of publishing.

Auden, W. H., *Collected Poems*, ed. Edward Mendelson. New York: Random House, 1976. Auden's "Spain 1937" appeared in his *Collected Poems*, 1945, and other earlier books now out of print; its earliest printed version is reproduced in *The English Auden*, ed. Mendelson. New York: Random House, 1977.

Baraka, Imamu Amiri (LeRoi Jones), *Black Magic Poetry 1961-1967*. Indianapolis: Bobbs-Merrill, 1969.

Barker, George, *Collected Poems, 1930-1965*. New York: October House, 1965.

————, *Collected Poems, 1930-1955*. London: Faber & Faber, 1957.

Berryman, John, 77 *Dream Songs*. New York: Farrar, Straus & Giroux; London: Faber & Faber, 1964.

Blackburn, Paul, *Early Selected y Mas: Poems 1949-1966*. Los Angeles: Black Sparrow Press, 1972.

————, *Peire Vidal: Translations*. New York/Amherst: Mulch Press, 1972.

Brecht, Bertolt, *Selected Poems*, trans. H. R. Hays. New York: Harvest Books, 1971.

Clarke, Austin, *Mnemosyne Lay in Dust*. Chester Springs, Pa.: Dufour Press; Dublin: Dolman Press; London: Oxford University Press, 1966.

Crane, Hart, *Complete Poems and Selected Letters and Prose*. New York: Liveright, 1966; London: Oxford University Press, 1968.

Dickinson, Emily, *The Poems of Emily Dickinson*. Cambridge: Harvard University Press, 1958; London: Faber & Faber, 1970.

Eliot, T. S., *Collected Poems 1909-1962*. New York: Harcourt Brace Jovanovich; London: Faber & Faber, 1963.

Fearing, Kenneth, *New and Selected Poems*. Bloomington: Indiana University Press, 1956.

Frost, Robert, *The Poetry of Robert Frost*. New York: Holt, Rinehart and Winston, 1969; London: Jonathan Cape, 1971.

Goodman, Paul, *Collected Poems*. New York: Random House, 1973.

Graves, Robert, *Collected Poems, 1965*. New York: Doubleday; London: Cassell, 1965.

Guthrie, Ramon, *Maximum Security Ward*. New York: Farrar, Straus & Giroux, 1970; London: Sidgwick & Jackson, 1971.

Hughes, Ted, *Crow*. New York: Harper & Row; London: Faber & Faber, 1971.

Jarrell, Randall, *The Complete Poems*. New York: Farrar, Straus & Giroux, 1969; London: Faber & Faber, 1971.

Kinnell, Galway, *The Book of Nightmares*. Boston: Houghton Mifflin, 1971.

Kinsella, Thomas, *Notes from the Land of the Dead*. New York: Knopf, 1973; Dublin: Cuala Press, 1972.

Lawrence, D. H., *The Complete Poems*. New York: Viking Press, 1964; London: Heinemann, 1971.

Lowell, Robert, *Life Studies*. New York: Farrar, Straus & Giroux, 1959; London: Faber & Faber, 1969.

Mayakovsky, Vladimir, *The Bedbug and Selected Poetry*, ed. Patricia Blake. New York: Meridian Books, 1960. "The Cloud in Trousers" was translated by George Reavey.

Moore, Marianne, *The Complete Poems*. New York: Macmillan/Viking, 1967; London: Faber & Faber, 1968.

Muir, Edwin, *Collected Poems*. New York: Oxford University Press, 1965; London: Faber & Faber, 1964.

Neruda, Pablo, *Estravagario*. Buenos Aires: Losada, 1958. My translation of "*La sirena y los borrachos*" appears in the present volume for the first time.

Owen, Wilfred, *The Collected Poems*. New York: New Directions, 1959; London: Chatto & Windus, 1964.

Pasternak, Boris, *Safe Conduct*, trans. Beatrice Scott. New York: New Directions, 1958.

Plath, Sylvia, *Ariel*. New York: Harper & Row, 1966; London: Faber & Faber, 1965.

Pound, Ezra, *The Cantos*. New York: New Directions, 1970; London: Faber & Faber, 1964. (Not identical editions.)

Rich, Adrienne, *The Will to Change*. New York: W. W. Norton, 1971; London: Chatto & Windus, 1973.

Rukeyser, Muriel, *Breaking Open*. New York: Random House, 1973.

Sassoon, Siegfried, *Collected Poems, 1908-1956*. New York: Viking Press; London: Faber & Faber, 1961.

Stevens, Wallace, *Collected Poems*. New York: Knopf, 1954; London: Faber & Faber, 1955.

Vergil, *The Pastoral Poems (The Eclogues)*, trans. E. V. Rieu. London: Penguin Books, 1949. Mr. Rieu uses the older spelling "Virgil" in this edition.

Williams, William Carlos, *The Collected Earlier Poems*. Norfolk, Conn.: New Directions, 1951; London: MacGibbon & Kee, 1967. Includes "Death" and "Love Song."

————, *Paterson*. New York: New Directions, 1963; London: MacGibbon & Kee, 1964.

Yeats, William Butler, *Collected Poems*. New York: Macmillan, 1956 ("Definitive Edition"); London: Macmillan, 1950.

Index of Quotations